Text Classics

PROFESSOR AFFERBECK LAUDER was the *nom de plume* of Alistair Morrison, who was born in Melbourne in 1911. After a brief stint at the National Gallery of Victoria Art School, he became interested in typographic design and started working as a graphic designer. In the early 1930s he moved to Sydney and then to London, where he immersed himself in the art scene and was an assistant to the Bauhaus great László Moholy-Nagy.

Returning to Sydney after the war, Morrison exhibited his abstract paintings in a number of shows, advised the state government on design matters and assisted the Reserve Bank in the design of decimal currency. In 1964, he invented Strine and—'quite by chance', he later recalled—began writing about it for the *Sydney Morning Herald*. He subsequently wrote the four Afferbeck Lauder books, illustrating them under his second *nom de plume*, Al Terego.

Let Stalk Strine and its successors were hugely popular, selling in the hundreds of thousands. Lauder became a household name and Strine entered the Australian consciousness, becoming a byword for the way we speak. Morrison, who always kept a lower profile than his creation ('an irritating but benevolent Frankenstrine monster'), moved to Fremantle, retired from design work and spent his last years painting. He died in 1998.

JOHN CLARKE is the author of numerous books, including *The Catastrophe Continues*, *The 7.56 Report*, *The Tournament*, *A Dagg at My Table* and *The Even More Complete Book of Australian Verse*. With Bryan Dawe, he has been performing satirical interviews on Australian television and radio since 1987. For less information, go to www.mrjohnclarke.com.

Strine
Afferbeck Lauder
illustrations by Al Terego

Text Publishing Melbourne Australia

The Text Publishing Company acknowledges the Traditional Owners of the country on which we work, the Wurundjeri people of the Kulin Nation, and pays respect to their Elders past and present.

Proudly supported by Copyright Agency's Cultural Fund.

textclassics.com.au
textpublishing.com.au

The Text Publishing Company
Wurundjeri Country, Level 6, Royal Bank Chambers, 287 Collins Street, Melbourne, Victoria 3000 Australia

Let Stalk Strine, *Nose Tone Unturned*, *Fraffly Well Spoke*n and *Fraffly Suite* first published in 1965, 1966, 1968 and 1969 by Ure Smith
This collection first published by The Text Publishing Company in 2009
This edition published 2012
Reprinted 2021

Cover, page design and typesetting by WH Chong
Cover illustrations by Al Terego

Printed in Australia by Griffin Press, an Accredited ISO AS/NZS 14001:2004 Environmental Management System printer

Primary print ISBN: 9781921922329
Author: Lauder, Afferbeck.
Title: Strine / by Afferbeck Lauder ; introduction by John Clarke.
Series: Text classics.
Subjects: English language--Australia. Australia--Humor.
Other Authors/Contributors: Clarke, John.
Dewey Number: 427.994

CONTENTS

Ford

by John Clarke

In the early 1960s the humour section in bookshops was very slender and had changed little since the Middle Ages. The selection contained especially few volumes relating to the experience, common to many of the citizens, of living in this part of the world. Then in 1965 a book appeared called *Let Stalk Strine*, apparently by Professor Afferbeck Lauder, explaining how to speak with an Australian accent. This important guide contained essential phrases such as 'How much is it?' 'Glorious home' and 'How are you going?' These and other useful expressions were translated from Strine into English, and the book quickly became compulsory; readings were conducted in Gloria Soames throughout the civilised world and a great many of the professor's observations were pressed into immediate usage, to general amusement on all sides.

It was a clever little book, distinctively illustrated by Al Terego and with typical conversations represented pictorially, as they would occur in real life. The title and the author's name ('Let's Talk Australian' by 'Professor Alphabetical Order') provided the clue, and once this was grasped sections could then be read out loud in the correct accent. This was one of the last hurrahs of parlour entertainment, once a feature of domestic life but by the late twentieth century eclipsed by radio and television. And it was all the work of the marvellous Alistair Morrison, who wrote the books in his fifties, with a mature and ironical perspective that provided an insight not just into the language but into the society it described.

Other volumes followed in short order: *Nose Tone Unturned* in 1966 and then two works about the more theatrical class of English pronunciation, *Fraffly Well Spoken* in 1968 and *Fraffly Suite* in 1969. The books were a publishing phenomenon. They were also a great enjoyment to a public hearing its own voice with growing confidence, and a sly social critique from Morrison, who specialised in the satirical equivalent of what police refer to as 'an inside job'.

The idea of setting phonetic spellings to the music of people's speech is a British comic tradition and was also much used by the performative, pre-Mark Twain American writers Artemus Ward and Petroleum V. Nasby. Morrison had a keen understanding of the forms he employed, among them the dictionary, the exam, verse, nursery rhymes, urban dialogue and sheet music. And although some of the cultural references have dated, the sharp eye and the instinct for mischief still provide enormous pleasure, whether you're on the Naw Shaw or in Kaimbra, whether you live in a Terror Souse or you're just the air fridge person.

Laze and Gem, Alistair Morrison.

LET STALK STRINE

LET STALK STRINE

A Lexicon of Modern Strine Usage
Compiled and Annotated by

Afferbeck Lauder

Professor of Strine Studies,
University of Sinny

Illustrated by *Al Terego*

About the Author

Afferbeck Lauder was born in Mairlben to humble parents of noble blood. He very early in life astounded his keeper by displaying his extraordinary gift for languages. When he was only two days old he could read Scrabble, and three days later he learned to speak Strine. His first words to his startled parents were, 'Hey, youse! Gimmier licker-ish trap an some chicken—an look, fellers, no hens.'

At the early age of three months he composed, and dedicated to his mother, the song entitled 'Thanks for the Mammary', which is still sung by Strines on Mother's Day. At the age of five he was appointed professor to the newly created School of Strine Studies at Ezz Rock.

Handicapped throughout his life by having been born with extreme myopia combined with a rare and curious malformation of what is believed to be his head, he was for many years unable to read or write without the aid of powerful trinoculars. His output, nevertheless, has been enormous. Publications include: 'Some Lesser-known Vowel Sounds among Cable Tram Gripmen', 'There Snow Datter Batcher—Yerron Yerrone' and 'Little Lauder's Lexicon'.

Asked about his hobbies, Professor Lauder replied, 'Well, I do have a hobby horse, but I'm really more interested in such simple pastimes as word-botching, wolf-whistling and just sin in the sun.'

Acknowledgments

The author expresses his grateful acknowledgments to the *Sydney Morning Herald*, in which much of the material in this book originally appeared. He would also like to thank the hundreds of *Herald* readers who so kindly wrote to him offering valuable criticism and advice, and who submitted so many unsolicited Strine words and phrases.

He would also like to express his warmest thanks to the following people, animals and things for their help in a variety of ways:

To the pioneers: C. J. Dennis and Colin Wills.

To Dr Breakface, for his generous and flattering foreword.

To his wife, who stood by him, no matter what they said; to his psychiatrist; to his goldfish; and to his dog, who answered the telephone and did all the typing.

And to the inventors and/or manufacturers of the following, without whose existence this book could never have been written: espresso coffee; Miltown; the lightweight telephone; anti-noise earplugs; money; *Roget's Thesaurus*; carbon paper; girls; and the little bits of cotton wool that they put in the tops of bottles of capsules.

Foreword

To have been asked by my good friend Afferbeck Lauder if I would consent to write a foreword to this erudite work is indeed a great honour. I have had the pleasure of knowing Professor Lauder for many years. We have, in fact, been very closely associated for so long, and have together been involved in so many projects of various kinds, that I think I may truthfully say that I have come to look upon him as my closest—indeed, one might say my only—friend.

As one would expect from a scholar of such brilliance and distinction, this, his latest work, is a truly remarkable publication. It is the result of many years of shrewd observation, patient research and hysterical insomnia. It is undoubtedly a work of great fatuity; aspersive yet inane; occasionally not even unpuerile; and, above all, minatory and warmly human.

This book cannot be called a 'heavy' work; in fact, quite the reverse—you will not be able to put it down. This perhaps is what makes it so remarkable; while following in the great tradition of Webster, Oxford and Roget, one is still able to carry it from room to room without inducing a hernia. I therefore commend it to you all—if you're still there.

Freud L. Breakface
'The Nutshell', Sydney, 1965

Introduction

It was recently reported* that while the English writer Monica Dickens was autographing copies of her latest book as they were being bought by members of the public in a Sydney shop, a woman handed her a copy and said, 'Emma Chisit.' Thinking that this was the woman's name, Monica Dickens wrote 'To Emma Chisit' above her signature on the flyleaf. The purchaser, however, in a rather more positive voice, said, 'No. Emma Chisit?' Eventually it became clear that she had been speaking Strine, and had used the Strine equivalent of the English phrase 'How much is it?'

The misunderstanding was due to the fact that Miss Dickens had never been told that while Strines are often able to understand and read English, they usually speak only Strine.

This incident made a profoundly disturbing impression on me. I realised that while we all speak Striné fluently and are able to understand each other without much difficulty, there did not seem to be any reliable and comprehensive dictionary of the language available for use by visitors, students, New Strines and people who speak only English.

It is obvious that incidents such as the above must cause endless misunderstanding, discord and international friction. This little book is an attempt partly to fill this gap.

---

* *Sydney Morning Herald*, 30 November 1964.

Let Stalk Strine

Air Fridge: A mean sum, or quantity; also: ordinary, not extreme. As in: The air fridge person; the air fridge man in the street.

Airman: *see* Semmitch.

Airpsly Fair Billis: Quite pleasant (*see also* Naw Shaw).

Airp's Trek: Mon painting in the ark ellery (*see also* Contempry).

Aorta: The English language contains many Greek, Latin, French, Italian and other foreign words, e.g. valet, vampire, vaudeville, vox-humana, hippocrepiform, etc. Strine, similarly, is richly studded with words and phrases taken from other, older tongues. Many of these have, with the passage of time, come to possess meanings completely different from their original ones. Two typical examples are the German words Eiche (pronounced *i-ker*; meaning oak-tree) and Ersatz (pronounced *air-sarts*; meaning substitute). Both these are now Strine words, and are used in the following manner: 'Eiche nardly bleevit,' and 'Ersatz are trumps, dear, yegottny?'

However, it is English which has contributed most to the Strine vocabulary. Strine is full of words which were originally English. Aorta is a typical example.

Aorta (pronounced *A-orta*) is the vessel through which courses the lifeblood of Strine public opinion. Aorta is a composite but nonexistent Authority which is held responsible for practically everything unpleasant in the Strine way of life; for the punishment of criminals; for the weather; for the Bomb and the Pill; for all public transport; and for all the manifold irritating trivia of everyday living. Aorta comprises the Federal and State legislatures; local government councils; all public services; and even, it is now thought, Parents and Citizens' Associations and the CSIRO.

Aorta is, in fact, the personification of the benevolently paternal welfare State to which all Strines—being fiercely independent and individualistic—appeal for help and comfort in moments of frustration and anguish.

The following are typical examples of such appeals. They reveal the innate reasonableness and sense of justice which all Strines possess to such a marked degree:

'Aorta build another arber bridge. An aorta stop half of these cars from cummer ninner the city—so a feller can get twirkon time.'

'Aorta mica laura genst all these prairlers and sleshers an pervs. Aorta puttem in jile an shootem.'

'Aorta stop all these transistors from cummer ninner the country. Look what they're doone to the weather. All this rine! Doan tell me it's not all these transistors—an all these hydrigen bombs too. Aorta stoppem!'

'Aorta have more buses. An aorta mikem smaller so they don't take up half the road. An aorta put more seats innem so you doan tefter stann all the time. An aorta have more room innem—you carn tardly move innem air so crairded. Aorta do something about it.'

Ark Ellery: *see* Airp's Trek.

Arm Arm: A child's appeal to its-mother for help. As in: 'Arm arm, makim stop.'

Ashfelt: Asphalt.

Assprad: Excessively preoccupied with domestic order and cleanliness. As in: 'She's very assprad—she keeps Rome looking lovely.'

This is a feminine adjective only; there does not appear to be any exact masculine equivalent, although the noun Hairndiman conveys something of the same meaning. Strine women may be assprad; Strine men may be hairndimen, or 'clever with their hens'. (*See also* Gloria Soame.)

Water bat
jars-chewer nigh
Goa
natter teat night?
Jarssa touvers.
Wicker deffer
few drinxer
Nairn F. T.

Well
I doan fee
larp twit treely.
I beenin
tair nawl die.
Hair bat
chew calmer nova
to mipe lice?
Wicked F. Teat
mipe lice

Baked Necks: A popular breakfast dish. Others include emma necks; scremblex; and fright shops.

Bandry: Marking a limit, or border. As in: 'Yadder job as a bandry rider.'

Bare Jet: A phrase from the esoteric sub-language spoken by Strine mothers and daughters. As in:
Q: 'Jim makier bare jet, Cheryl?'
A: 'Narm arm, nar chet.'

Bim-Bye: To have been attacked. As in: 'Arm, arm, I've bin bim-bye a bull joe'; or 'He was having a laidan when he was bim-bye a fahl-web spider.'

Blue, Hala: Famous Strine soprano. Hala Blue and Andy Kleimags first appeared together as a light opera team in 1907 in *Snow White and the 700 Decibels*. Since that time, until the outbreak of television and the subsequent merciful decline of musical comedy, this ever-popular team has captured the hearts of Strine audiences whenever they appeared.

Even 'Old Vienna' type productions could not dampen the enthusiasm of their many faithful fans. Hala Blue as La Stentoretta in *The Shriek and the Cholera Tourer* was, to put it mildly, unforgettable.

For seventeen years this talented couple successfully toured the country, playing always to packed houses, in the roles of Dr Yes and Little Miss Noma in 'Mam Barfly and Ida'.

Boll; Boller: Glass container with narrow neck; e.g. A boller brosser pearl; a sick sands boll; less cracker boll, etc.

Bran: A dark, brannish colour. Rairping piper is usually bran, as also are bombers in Sinny.

Chair Congeal: Bisexual adhesive used in making furniture. First mentioned in early Strine nursery-rhyme science fiction. Unfortunately it is not possible to reproduce here the unexpurgated version of the rollicking old ballad which has been handed down to us from the earthy, uninhibited people of earlier days. At the request of the Strine Literary Censorship Vigilance Committee, blanks have been substituted for certain passages which might have offended the sensibilities of modern Strines.

> Chair congeal went up the hill,
> Blank, blank and blank with laughter,
> Blank, blank and blank; but blank—the Pill.
> Congeal came tumbling after.

Cheque Etcher: Did you obtain. As in: 'Where cheque etcher hat?' or 'Where cheque etcher dim pull, sonny? Where cheque etcher big blue wise?'

Cheque Render: An ornamental tree with blue flares.

Contempry: Mon painting, furniture, architecture, etc. As in: 'I'd have the aqua, Bev, it's more contempry.' Note: Airp's trek, contempry, mon and sreelist are all more or less synonymous and interchangeable terms.

Corpse: *see* Harps.

Cummer Ninner: *see* Aorta.

Dare Debts: No-hopers; nark leds; rep bairgs; drongoes.

Deteriate: To grow worse, or inferior; to deteriorate.

Didgerie: A prefix, the exact meaning of which depends on the suffix which follows. This suffix is usually: do, dabat, or lee-meenit. As in:
  (a) Man, he plays the didgerie do real good.
  (b) Didgerie dabat it in the piper?
  (c) Didgerie lee-meenit or were you kidding?

Dimension: The usual response to 'Thenk you' or 'Thenk, smite.'

Dingo: A word with two separate, unrelated meanings. When intoned with equal emphasis on the syllables it is the negative response to the question 'Jeggoda?' As in:

Q: Jeggoda the tennis?

A: Nar, dingo. Sorten TV.

When, however, the emphasis is on the first syllable, dingo becomes a parliamentary term of mild reproof.

Dismal Guernsey: Dollars and cents.

Doan Lemmyaf: I do not want to have to. As in: 'Arn jew kids in bare jet? Emeny times die affter tellyer. Now doan lemmyaf to speak dear Ken.'

Ear's Eve: The festive occasion of 31 December. Each year, at midnight, Strines throughout the land perform the ceremony of joining hands with strangers and chanting 'Shoulder Quaint's Beef Cot' (also known as 'Frolang Zine').

Ebb Tide: Hunger; desire for food. As in: 'I jess dono watser matter, Norm, I jess got no ebb tide these dyes.'

Egg Jelly: In fact; really. As in: 'Well, there's nothing egg jelly the matter with her. It's jess psychological.'

Egg Nishner: A mechanical device for cooling and purifying the air of a room.

Emeny: *see* Doan Lemmyaf; Enemy; and Semmitch.

Enemy: The limit of. As in: Enemy tether. Not to be confused with Emeny of the phrase 'Emeny jiwant?'

Eye-level Arch: The Strine method of ordering a meal in a restaurant. As in: 'Eye-level arch play devoisters Anna piner martyr sauce an tea,' or 'Eye-level arch ching chair min an some Swissair pork.'

Fair Plessen: *see* Naw Shaw.

Fillum: Film.

Fipes: *see* Harps.

Fitwer Smeeide; Fiwers Youide; Whinecha: (Synonyms) If I were you I would. As in: 'Fitwer smeeide leave him. He saw-way sonn the grog, Annie carn work wily strinken.' Or: 'Fiwers youide leave him, anide goan livner unit. He snore worthit trouble.' Or: 'Whinecha leave him. He'll nebby any good. You know your selfies no good. You carng gon frever like this.'

Flares: Blooms, blossoms; e.g. corn flares, wile flares, etc. As in:

> Q: Wet cheque ettha flares?
> A: Gloria sarnthay. I gom airtat Sairf Nils.

Flesh in the Pen: Momentary brilliance. As in: 'Ar, stoo gooder last, Sairndra, it's jessa flesh in the pen.' The derivation of this curious phrase is obscure. General etymological opinion is that it has come down from the time when the early Strine settlers fashioned pens from goose quills—often without first removing the goose. The phrase is believed originally to have been 'gooseflesh in the pen', meaning shaky or illegible writing (caused by the struggles of the goose).

Foo Fairies: Characters in a popular television commercial, 'Woo worse, Foo Fairies, the happy way to shop.'

Furry Tiles: Sick humour for kiddies. These are stories which begin with the words 'One spawner time', and then describe in graphic and revolting detail various acts of murder, mayhem and treachery, such as '…he drew out a sharp knife and cut off the head of the wicked brother,' and 'At nightfall they came to the edge of a deep forest and the young maiden then did what the witch had told her—she cut out the young huntsman's heart and threw it down the well. Then she wept bitter tears and could not be comforted and they lived happily ever after.' Because of their violence and gloomy horror such stories are, naturally, very popular with young children, and it is surprising that so few Strine furry tiles exist. Those that do are usually variations on the theme of 'If we are returned to power…' or 'You may rest assured that I shall leave no stone unturned.'

Gadgeter: I would be most grateful if you would. As in: 'I'll gadgeter sew a bun ommy shirt,' or 'Yeggo ninter tan? I'll gadgeter gepme some lickerish traps an some rise-up lides.'

Garbler Mince: Within the next half hour. Also: Greetings. As in: 'I'll be with you in a garbler mince,' or 'With the garbler mince of the Gem of Directors.' (*See also* Gobbler Mincer.)

Garment: An invitation to visit. As in: 'Garment seamy anile seward icon do.' And: 'Garment the garden, Maud, I mirrored the gaiter loan.' —*Tennyson.*

Gest Vonner: Well-known linguist, heard regularly on the Ibey Sea. (*See also* Naw Shaw; and Slidy.)

Gissa: 'Please give me…' As in: 'Gissa lookcha alchbra.' This word is the subject of a curious sexual taboo; it may be used only by males. The female equivalent is Gimme, or Gimmier. As in: 'Gimmier nairm semmitchenna cuppa tea.'

Gloria Soame: A spurban house of more than fourteen squares, containing fridge, telly, wart wall carps, payshow and a kiddies' rumps room. Antonym: Terror Souse (*q.v.*).

Gobbler Mincer: Greetings. As in: The gobbler mincer the season. Or: With the gobbler mincer the author. (*See also* Garbler Mince.)

Gona Gota: To go. As in: 'They're gona gota Gundagai to get a gelding and they're gona gota gether.' Or:

    Q: You gona gota Moun Barflo freester?

    A: Narm gona gota Mairlben. I'm stain with some frenset Blair Crock.

Gonnie: Do you have any? As in: 'Gonnie epples?' 'Gonnie forby three oregon?' 'Gonnie news a Bev?'

Grade A: So-called 'fine' weather, i.e. an intolerably hot and blinding summer day; also, an important occasion. As in: 'It's a grade A for the Irish'; 'It's a grade A for the people of Fiver No'; 'It's a grade A for the Dairptic Mishner of Texation.'

Gunga Din: Locked out. As in:
> A: I gunga din, the door slokt.
> B: Hancher gotcher key?
> A: Air, buttit spoultered on the inside. I tellyer I gunga din. Car more, nope-nit.

Harps: Thirty minutes past the hour. As: Harps two; harps four; harps tait; etc. Related words are: Fipes; temps; corpse. As: Fipes one; temps two; corpse four.

Header, Mary: Daughter of one of the early Strine graziers. She was responsible, after years of bitter struggle with the authorities, for the introduction of compulsory education for sheep. She thus lit a lamp which has continued to burn steadily down the years and many of to-day's famous Strine sheep must be grateful to her memory. One of her little lambs, Charles, who had followed her to school each day, eventually became an essayist and poet of considerable skill and composed the following song in memory of his sponsor:

> Mary Header little lamb;
> An intellectual nit.
> It never passed its first exam
> Because it couldn't sit.
>
> So Mary Header little lamb
> With vegies and mint sauce.

Carmen F. T. Withers.
We revving
ching liffis.
Jellike ching liffis?
We F. N. B. Neffen
roe smeal slightly
wither tellion
the kitser nawl.
Yeckered
calm strife rom
work

Theng Saula Syme
butter monner
diet.
I fed a bitifer
gairstrick
stummick lightly.
Spin plier
nuppagenner bit.
Arlga mauve rafter.
Oliver
bye tweet first

'Oh, dearest lamb,' she cried, 'I am
As hungry as a horse.'

Hembairg: A bag, carried by all Strine women, for the transport of personal possessions such as money, cigarettes, lipstick and a hairnkie. (*See also* Wezzme.)

Hip Ride: Popular radio music. Note: Any tune played more than twice becomes known as 'heather hip ride' or 'numbwun hip ride'.

Hop Eyes: Pastry cases, containing gravy, and occasionally heated. The singular is hop eye, or hoppine sauce.

I Marfter: I am about to leave. As in: 'Well, I marfter tan now. I'll gadgeter turn the oven on at harps four,' and 'I marfter see the Wizard.' (*See also* Gona Gota.)

Inner Narkup Luddaze: A builder's term, meaning: within the next seven or eight weeks. An elaboration of this phrase, 'Air smite, inner narkup luddaze for sure,' means, in the building trade, within the next seven or eight weeks.

Jans: An opportunity. As in: 'He neffradder jans,' or 'He neffrad Barclay's jans.'

Jareedna; Wairtsed: These terms, relating to the dissemination of news, cannot be translated individually as they always occur in close juxtaposition in conversations such as the following:

Q: Jareedna piper wairtsed abat the bushfires? (or: abat the universty stewnce?)
A: Nar, sorten TV. (or: sorten *Woomz Dye*.)

Jeep Yo: A large building in each capital city. Administered by the Peem Jeeze Department of the Commwealth Garment.

Jess Tefter; Lefter: It is necessary to. As in: 'She'll jess tefter get chews twit,' or 'You lefter filner form.'

Jezz: Articles of furniture. As in: 'Set the tible, love, and get a coupler jezz.'

Kelly, Ned ('Our Ned'): A notorious artists' model. Also thought to have been a bushranger.

Laidan: A short rest after the midday meal; a siesta.

Larks, Girldie: Research into early Strine history and the origins of the Strine language has continued to yield a rich harvest. Creeping about and sneezing among the foetid pages of old manuscripts; listening at the keyholes of the better-informed; surreptitiously removing pages from public library books—all these activities, though necessary, are exhausting and dangerous. But to the dedicated searcher after truth the rewards more than make up for the hardships. Such a reward has been the recent chance discovery of the true facts about Girldie Larks and the Forebears, now told here for the first time.

Girldie Larks was an early Strine juvile dinquent tea nature, whose scandalous career has until now been hushed up and whose evil character was whitewashed by her sentimental, over-indulgent parents. Girldie Larks is now known to have been a psychopathic thief and tormentor of dumb animals. An associate of Little Red Robin and other hoods, she made the lives of our forebears intolerable by her continual raids into their territory—trespassing, stealing food and destroying property.

Her special victims appear to have been the upright and popular Behr family—Father, Mother, Baby and the silent and rather less well-known Cammom Behr. Her savage depredations continued for some years until eventually, his patience exhausted, Cammom cried, 'A little Behr will fix her!' and he then cut out her heart and threw it down a well—this being the appropriate course of action in those days when there were so many wells about. (*See also* Furry Tiles.)

A typical example of Girldie Larks' vicious cruelty is immortalised in the following old Strine folk song:

Girldie Larks, Girldie Larks, where have you been?
I beat up London and vented my spleen,
And then I cummome menai harassed the Behrs;
I yay tarp their porridge and bro karp their chairs.
I savaged the beds and I tordan the fences
And frightened a little mouse out of its senses.

Laze and Gem: Usual beginning of a public speech. Often combined with Miss Gem. As in: 'Miss gem, laze and gem. It gives me grape leisure…'

Lenth: Length.

Letty Mare Fit: Let him have it. As in: 'Letty mare fit tiffy wonsit. Zarf trawly zonier kid.'

Lickerish: Licorice.

Londger Ray: Women's underclothing.

Major, the Big Horse-cart: The Strine patron saint of young married couples, or as they are sometimes indulgently known, 'nearlyweds'. How the big horse-cart major came to acquire his curious nickname is unknown; indeed much of his life and background is obscured by conflicting reports and cryptic half-truths. One thing, however, is certain and that is that he has always been associated with marriage and weddings. Today no self-respecting soloist at a Strine wedding can be restrained from singing that so well-loved melody addressed to 'Big Horse-cart Major Mine'.

An ashy wonster
doop the sperrume
an the lairnge.

Enchy storkner bat
a rumps room.

It carng gon
marsh lonker.

Washy thing
kiam?

Weller
corset snop
my bizner sreely
but jeer
fiwers youide
poomy foot dairn
nide
teller weshie
get sawf

Mare Chick: Effects produced by the assistance of supernatural powers. As in: Bleck mare chick; mare chick momence; 'Laugh, your mare chick spell is airfree ware.'

Marmon Dead: Parents. As in: 'I saw Marmon dead, Sandra, they'd love tier frommier.'

Miss Gem: Correct method of addressing a person chairing a meeting.

Money: The day following Sunny. (Sunny, Money, Chewsdy, Wensdy, Thursdy, Fridy, Sairdy.)

Nardly; Carn Tardly: *see* Aorta.

Naw Shaw: A district of suburban Sinny, extending from Klahra to Waitara.

Naw Shaw is also a dialect of Strine, very closely related to the dialects spoken at Trairk, Sath Yeah, Poym Piper and Rare Dill in Kairmbra. Gest Vonner, the overseas visiting linguist, speaks fluent Naw Shaw. 'Airpsly Fair Billis' is a typical Naw Shaw phrase, meaning: Quite pleasant, or mildly enjoyable. Another interesting Naw Shaw term is 'Fair Plessen', which means much the same thing, as in: 'Oat wess mosen choiple—wee etta fair plessen Dane deed.'

Neffereffer: Never. As in: 'He neffereffer rurdafit.' Sometimes: Nefferefffereven. As in: 'The referee nefferefffereven nurda wordavit.'

Nerve Sprike Tan: Mental collapse due to conflict, anxiety, etc. As in: 'He never let sarp, marm. He'll ever nerve sprike tan the waze goane.'

Nipey: *see* Split nair dyke.

Numb Butter; Jessa: (Synonyms) Only. As in: 'They're numb butter buncher drongoes,' or 'He's jessa nohoper.'

Orpheus Rocker: Psychopathic; neurotic; psychotic; slow; quick;

eccentric; absent-minded; unstable; excitable; imaginative; introspective; creative; or in any way different.

Panam: Unit of weight. As in: A panam inn smeat.

Porchy, George E.: The main character in one of those baffling and inconsequent nursery rhymes with which Strine parents have for so long brainwashed their unfortunate children. Nauseatingly coy and yet loaded with disturbing ambiguity, it has been conceived with the obvious intention of engendering a sense of bewildered insecurity in the psyche of the innocent child. For those who are unfamiliar with the rhyme, the authorised version is as follows:

> George E. Porchy kissed the girls and made them cry
> And doesn't know where to find them.
> And his bullets were made of lead, lead, lead,
> And cockle shells all in a row.

Note the unhealthy emphasis on sex—presented as something terrifying, something which makes one cry. Note the equivocal melancholy of 'doesn't know where to find them'. Note the neo-colonial imperialistic line about bullets; and finally those cockle shells—all in a row like a lot of undemocratic automata.

Surely this is calculated to corrupt and deprave. Surely children should be told only the clean, straightforward, realistic tales of violence and horror that their little minds crave, and which fit them so well for the world of today. All this provocative and menacing symbolism of bullets and cockle shells must surely induce nightmares and must inhibit the normal kicking of playmates' shins and the happy gouging out of little eyes.

Fortunately, recent research into early Strine history has brought to light important new facts about George E. Porchy. He was, in fact, just

Noppaired.

Euro merli. Jeck seddy

Wez Jeck? woonker min.

I thorty scona Seddiwer slight.

geminner neffer He's

drink. jar sporter

Whyndie geminnen Noel toonar

silo fleeter

eneffer drink? with twink arbies

N. Hair jigger anorlat

tonn? chairs

a lovable old poisoner and a great favourite of little girls everywhere. This means that the whole squalid incident of the cockle shells can be forgotten, and the rhyme rewritten somewhat as follows:

George E. Porchy kissed the girls
And wrapped them round with furs and pearls.
He stroked their cheeks and called them 'Honey'
And gave them little bags of money.
He gave them cognac with their coffee,
And, finally, some homemade 'toffee'.
He said, as rigor mortis followed,
'It must be something that they swallowed.'

Giorgio Eduardo Porchy was the only son of Allegro and Lucrezia Borgia, who migrated from Italy to this country in 1852, where they changed their name to Porchy and established a small poisoning and garrotting shop in a prosperous goldmining town near Bendigo.

Giorgio, a bright boy with a happy nature, took to poisoning effortlessly. When he was twelve both his parents died suddenly in rather mysterious circumstances, and he immediately took over the shop, which he rapidly built up into a thriving business.

For a while he had a little trouble with the authorities, who tended to be rather conservative in their ways. Fortunately, however, the police sergeant and the local magistrate were both women—the handsome Durberville sisters, daughters of the local dairyman. This no doubt is the origin of the preposterous libel about 'kissed the girls and made them cry over spilt milk'. Anyway, the likeable young George soon won their hearts and married them. He soon inherited the dairy from their father, who had passed away unexpectedly an hour or so after the wedding breakfast, and he successfully combined the two businesses.

Eventually he became mayor, then local member, and finally a senator, and was for many years one of the most popular figures in the district.

After his murder the local citizens, whose number had by this time dwindled to about twenty-five, erected a monument to his memory in the form of a bronze statue holding aloft a smoking test tube, and surrounded by a group of happy little girls waving arsenical lipsticks. Issuing from his smiling lips is an elegant bronze 'balloon' on which is inscribed his family motto: 'Spero non Taedium'—I hope I haven't Borgia.

Puck, Charlie Charm: A whimsical character in Strine folklore, about whom many amusing anecdotes are told. Charlie Puck is famous for having introduced the popular sport of sheep-stealing. Mentioned in the national anthem ('Where sat Charlie Charm Puck you've got in your tucker bag?').

Rare Dill: A district in Kairmbra.

Rare Wick: A suburb of Sinny; also a racecourse.

Rep Bairg: An irresponsible person. (*See also* Dare Debts.)

Retrine: Making an effort. As in: How to speak Strine without re-trine.

Ridinghood, Red: An attractive auburn-haired young woman who lived in a bark hut on the goldfields during the 1850s. At the time of the following incident she was unmarried but had a middle-aged friend who used to visit her regularly because his plain, elderly wife didn't understand him. This friend was a bit of an old wolf. He wore well-polished handmade shoes and had long teeth and pointed ears, but he was kind to Red and used to give her presents, and always paid the rent of the hut, to which he had his own key. Red used to call him 'Wolfie' and 'Daddy', and tried not to yawn when he talked about himself and about what he had said to the Minister.

One day Red came home from a visit to her furrier and found her friend sitting up in bed with a shawl covering his head and face, leaving only his teeth and chins visible. Surprised, because she couldn't remember having seen the shawl before, Red said, 'What's the matter, Big Daddy? You got near acre somethink?'

'I think I musta picked up a virus, dear,' came the muffled, slightly falsetto reply. 'Also, me teeth are falling out, one after another—oops, there goes another one!'—and a large, gamboge canine tooth fell onto the bed, where it lodged upright, quivering like a dagger.

Alarmed, but not yet suspicious, Red cried out, 'Gee, Wolfie, yorter tiger nipey sea or somethink.' But the figure on the bed beckoned to her: 'No, thanks, dear, jusker meeren help me back with this tooth.'

Red, suspicious, drew back in alarm. She was almost sure now that this creature was an intruder and, worse still, probably female. There was a tense silence for a few moments. Then Red moved quickly. Knowing that her life probably depended on speed; knowing that, momentarily, she held the advantage; certain at last that this was an impostor and knowing that there could be no substitute for wolf, she sprang at the menacing old doll on the bed and gave her a brisk clip over the left ear with an empty sherry bottle.

It was all over in seconds. The last of the teeth fell away, taking the shawl with them, and revealing the pitiful, cowering figure of her friend's plain, elderly wife.

'Don't hit me again, dear,' she whined. 'I didn't mean any harm. I was on me way to the dentist—I've had a lot of trouble with me teeth and that lately. You know how it is out here—nothing but damper and salt beef and that—no vegies or anything. Anyway, zize saying, I was on me way to the dentist when I had one of me turns like, and I thought I'd come in and have a bit of a laidan till it passed. I didn't think you'd mind. I must have dropped off. Ooh, you must think I'm awful.'

She paused, smiled wanly at Red, and picked a piece of glass out of her ear. 'We haven't seen you for such a long time, dear,' she went on. 'Whine cher comoveren have tea with us one day soon. I was zony sane to Norm lar snite, you know, Norm, we oughter ask Red to co-moveren have tea with us. The poor kid must be lonely all by herself in that hut and all.'

Red breathed more easily as her fears ebbed away. The old girl hadn't found out, then, about her friendship with Norm. She picked her way through the broken glass and teeth and helped her victim to her feet. 'Gee, Elsie, I'd no idea it was you. I'm real sorry. Lep me getcher a cuppa tea.' She fussed over her, covered her ear with bandaids and took her round to the dentist.

Norm never came to see Red again, and after a few weeks she got a letter from the agent about the rent. But then Norm had always been frightened that people would find out that there might be a scandal and he wouldn't be re-elected. Norm had always been so kind, though. Red was lonely for a while, but not for long—there were plenty of other wolves about on the goldfields in those days.

Rigid VI: Early Strine king; sometimes called Quick Brown Fox or Tete d'Oeuf (or Rigid Egg-head). Rigid the Sixth was a devoted husband and father, and was also very fond of animals, in marked contrast to his predecessors, who had spent most of their spare time shooting arrows into the wild bores who roamed the palace corridors.

Rigid was also something of an eccentric; he invariably spoke English to his subjects but tolerantly allowed them to reply in their native Strine tongue. This democratic monarch's sense of justice was so fastidious that he treated even the royal alphabet with scrupulous fairness, and whenever he spoke always allowed each letter to make at least one brief appearance. The following scene from Act II of *Rigid VI* reveals the confusion which occasionally resulted from this curious habit.

Scene: The palace moat, dry now because of the continual drought. Enter: Rigid and John, carrying bags of superphosphate. From Rigid's golden crown hangs a row of little corks on strings. His companion brushes away the flies with a small branch of mulga. Both look hot and uncomfortable in their purple velvet robes.

Rigid: The quick brown fox jumps over the lazy dog.

John: What dog, your mare-chesty? Snow dog ear mite.

Rigid: Rigid the Sixth briefly views Jack's pink zombi quins.

John: Wasser matter with you, King? That was muncer go— and stop jumping, will yer. Snow dog ear, I tellya—Give yer the creeps.

Rigid: Quiet gadfly jokes with six vampire cubs in zoo.

John: Gaudy scone office rocker. Listen, King, zoos hev neffereffer even been inventor jet.

Rigid: King Rigid and Queen Zoe believe the wolf may expect jams.

John: That sawright, King, we should have plennier jammer tome. Mine jew, the quins get through a coupla jars every dye, though. Would golden syrup do? What wolf?

Rigid: Jumpy zebra vows to quit thinking coldly of sex.

John: Jeez, so now we got zebras too. No wonder they're gonna hafter invent zoos. Look out, King, jump! It's that dog again.

Rigid: Two fixed androgynes doze quickly on film job. I have spoken.

Exeunt, humming 'Waltzing Matilda' and cracking gold-handled stockwhips.

Rise Up Lides: Sharpened steel wafers, now usually stineless, used for shiving.

Rye-Wye: A dialect spoken by the Trine tribe. Strine, like any other living language, is constantly changing as new words and phrases are evolved or introduced and as old ones fall into disuse. All languages, and Strine is no exception, also carry with them many local dialects and sub-languages.

These are usually more conservative than the mother tongue. Like the side eddies in a river, they remain static and self-contained—almost unaffected by the main stream of the language—and thus they become increasingly cryptic and obscure.

Such a dialect is Rye-Wye, which is spoken only by the Trine tribes over the public address systems of metropolitan railway stations.

All attempts to decipher this esoteric dialect have so far been unsuccessful, and it is now believed that it is not understood even by the Trine tribes who speak it. Rye-Wye is, in short, a ritualistic chant, the purpose of which is not to inform but to frighten away any passengers or other hostile spirits who may be lurking in the underground. For this reason it is not only terrifyingly loud but also breathtakingly dissonant. The following are typical examples:

(a) 'Awe lathers trine nair stannenat num-rye teen plafform pliz. Istrine term night sear. Awe lattpliz.'

(b) 'Nuffor plafform nawshawtrine stomming milce point naw sinny chasswood norl staish toresby.'

(c) 'Trine num-rye teen plafform gerster rare fern, bird and strair feel lonely.'

Sag Rapes: Anything which one wants but is unable to reach.

Sander's Lape: In a state of suspended animation. As in: 'Doan mica noise, Norm, the kiddies are Sander's lape.'

Saw Bat: Past tense of the verb to read. As in: 'I saw bat it in *Pix*,' or 'I saw bat it in Sairdy's piper.'

Scared Saul: Mythical hero. Believed to have been the originator and spiritual head of the Boy Scat movement. This movement, so popular with Strines and New Strines alike, embraces also the Gurgides, Sea Scats, Brannies and Carbs. Scared Saul (known to his intimates as Jobber Bob) is thought to have been in some way related to Gloria Sarah Titch (*q.v.*). The meeting place and local centre of Scat activity is known everywhere today as the Scared Saul.

Fune Mervered
like tucker
mofer
wah neefnink
we'd laugh to see you.
Jekyll
show yiz slides.
An we gossamer
Wendy skitty stoo

G-weed
laughter seam.
Butter dunnif
wickairn.
Altar pants
on Merv.
E. Sconofer seesoon
N. U. Nairtiz
snore
flotta do

Scettin Lairder: It is becoming louder. (*See also* Scummin Glerser.)

Scona: A meteorological term. As in: Scona rine; scona clear up; scona be a grade A; etc.

Scummin Glerser: Approaching. As in:

> Q: Jeer that noise, Norm? Wodger reckna tiz? What everit tiz, scettin lairder—scummin glerser.
>
> A: Tsawright, dear, tsonia wisspring jet.

Semmitch: Two slices of bread with a filling in between, e.g. M-semmitch; semmon semmitch; chee semmitch. When ordering semmitches the following responses are indicated:

> A: Sell semmitches?
>
> B: Air, emeny jiwant?
>
> A: Gimmie utter martyr and an airman pickle. Emma chisit? (or: Emma charthay?)
>
> B: Toon nimepen slidy. (or: Threen form smite. A man is always expected to pay more for food than a woman is.)

Sex: Large cloth bags used as containers for such things as potatoes, cement, etc. As in: Sex of manure, corn sex, etc. Also known as heshing bairgs.

Shablay: Chablis.

Share: Bathroom water spray. As in: 'Wine chevver cole share?' or 'I think I'll ever shy venner not share.' Also: Rain. As in: Scadded shares and thunnerstorms.

Sick Snite: *see* Soup-marked Money.

Slidy; Smite: The feminine and masculine suffixes of the terms 'Theng slidy' and 'Theng smite' (meaning: Thank you, madam, and Thank you, sir). It is interesting to compare these terms with a similar one used by Gest Vonner and other overseas visitors—Thairnk yoch. As in: 'Thairnk yoch for the orp tune tare…' (*See also* Naw Shaw.)

Sly Drool: An instrument used by engineers for discovering Kew brutes and for making other calculations.

Smarfit, Lilma: Early Strine health faddist and fetch-terrian. While still in her teens Miss Lilma Smarfit inherited the huge Smarfit chain of health-food stores—retail distributors of curds, whey, apple vinegar and molasses. Uncompromising in her love of vegetables and by nature obsessively ruminative, she devoted her long life to the cause of fetch-terrianism. Many nursery rhymes have been written about her exploits. The following is perhaps the best known:

> Lilma Smarfit sat on a tarfit,
> Digesting a bushel of hay.
> She cried, 'I'm a bird
> Who's addicted to curd,
> And I'm to be Queen of the Whey.'

In spite of her fierce devotion to cellulose and dairy produce, Lilma Smarfit is known to have been an associate and consort of such gourmets and voluptuaries as little Jack 'Thumbs' Horner and George E. Porchy.

Snow White and the Severed Wharves: Snow White was a beautiful young Strine secret-service agent. In private life she was a doctor of philosophy and a connoisseur of immersion heating. As a counter-spy (officially known as 004), she was noted for her dexterity with the hypodermic syringe and for her unswerving promiscuity in the service of her country.

Her most remarkable attributes, however, were her extraordinarily powerful lungs, which she used to great advantage whenever mouth-to-mouth anti-resuscitation was the only way to escape from the embraces of a no-longer-useful admirer. This high-pressure method was rather frowned on by her more conservative colleagues but it was undeniably effective; her victim just dilated like a sunfish and became entangled in the chandeliers, or drifted over the horizon in whatever direction the wind happened to be blowing.

It was a dull, grey autumn afternoon when Snow White left the Colonel's office. She stepped into her rollerskates, and picked her way carefully through the traffic to the middle of the road. Skating along the centre line of a main highway usually calmed her turbulent spirit and gave her a sense of purpose and fulfilment. But today, somehow, she felt troubled and uneasy.

The Colonel's warning was still ringing in her ears. 'No more lust, Buster, I trust you. It's a must,' he had said, putting down the rhyming dictionary and lighting her cigar. 'Carry two Mausers in your trousers, and pack a new Luger with the nougat.'

Snow White knew what lay behind that friendly half-smile which contrasted so oddly with his grey, intelligent eyes, obscured now by the large empty prune can with which he always concealed his face from his subordinates. Poor James, she thought, how sensitive he still is about having no nose. His voice droned on: '...and your teeth will be sharpened before you leave. That is all.' He paused and spoke a few words into the intercom.

He had briefed her well, she thought to herself as she overtook a large black sedan filled with Asians carrying cameras. Her mission was simple, but dangerous. She was to make her way undetected into 'their' territory, destroy the fleet of mini-submarines and cut loose the floating wharves at Vitamin Bay. That was all. Simple enough, heaven knows—yet her uneasiness persisted.

Suddenly she threw away her cigar, put out her right arm and pulled sharply into the kerb at the left. She made her way thoughtfully towards a small, unobtrusive building which bore a large sign: 'Day Old Pullets—Hot Water—Ears Bashed Wile-U-Wate—Cocker Puppies—Clean Toilets—Devonshire Teas.' She rapped on the boarded-up window with a rollerskate. 'Are you there, James?' she called softly. There

Sarn's
calmer nairt.
Scona beer
gloria sty.
Mine jute still
scold zephyr.
Cheat was scold
la snite

Weller corset
Saul-wye school
linnermore
ninx.
Buttered swarm
nuddite-time.
Spewffle
climb a treely

was no answer. She went round to the locked door, put her lips to the keyhole and blew out the lock. She stepped quietly inside. The Colonel was already there. She took him in her strong arms and kissed him fiercely on the prune can immediately above the words 'Contains no preservatives'. He snuggled close to her and gurgled tinnily. She took his hand and together they walked along the narrow catwalk towards the submarines.

Snow White patted the Luger inside her armpit and sniffed cautiously at the outgoing tide. There wouldn't be much time, she thought. She bent down and bit through the first cable with her powerful teeth, and watched the grey hull sink slowly out of sight into the mud.

She looked around her. It was almost dark now, and the Colonel appeared to be asleep. She smiled grimly as she scrabbled among the barnacles, searching for the second cable. Suddenly, without warning, a blinding light flashed into her eyes and a suave, unctuous voice broke the silence: 'Weaner rup this sprogram to bring you an important annancement from the Sinny Cricket Grand. New Sath Wiles are orlat for three unren twen yite.' The menacing voice chilled her, and her hand gripped the Luger. 'The forecast for tomorrow is for scadded shares and Sathie's twins. An now we return you to this chewdio.' There was a click, then silence. Once more she was in darkness.

She was alone now; the Colonel had disappeared. At last she found the second cable and sank her teeth into the steel. The oily water closed over the last of the wharves. Her mission was completed.

Through a little window in the wrist of her black rubber frogwoman's suit she saw that it was only two hours since she had left the Colonel's office. She felt her way through the dark hut to the doorway, and out into the chill mountain air. She carefully adjusted her skates, pulled out from the kerb and made for the centre line of the road.

She smiled gently in the darkness, and switched on her tail-light. It was, she thought as she spat out a few shreds of cable, good—she paused and lit a cigar—to be—as James would say—alive.

Soup-marked Money: The language of prices of goods sold in a soup-marked, or self-service grocery. The following are typical examples: fawn ten; fawn tum sipenee; nime-pen soff; sick snite; tairmpen soff; tumce, etc. These terms are of particular interest to the historian, as they will disappear with the introduction of dismal guernsey, after which time all prices will be expressed in dolls and sense.

Spargly Guys: *see* Tiger.

Spin-ear Mitch: Much alike; closely resembling one another. As in: 'He's the spin-ear mitch of his old man.'

Split Nair Dyke: A continual sensation of pain in the head. As in: 'I got a split nair dyke. Smor niken bear; I left a tiger nipey sea.'

Spoultered: *see* Gunga Din.

Star Ginter: *see* Stark Ender.

Stark Ender: (Or, occasionally, Star Ginter.) An enthusiastic attack. As in: 'They all got stark ender the grog on Ear's Eve.'

Stewnce: Persons engaged in learning something from books, or attending an educational institution, especially of the higher class; scholars; persons dedicated to the pursuit of knowledge. As in: Four stewnce were arrested and charged with offensive behaviour. Or: Plea sledge stewnce threw Exeter bystanner.

Swice, Swy: So I. As in: 'Swice settwer wine chermine cherrone business, I settwer snunner your business wad-eye do.' Or: 'Swy roe twim an I toldim jus wad-eye thorter fim. Oy's a sarder sniles.'

Tan Cancel: The elected local government authority.

Tea Nature: *see* Girldie Larks.

Teedo, Dorimy Fasola: World-famous lyricist and soprano. Strines have every reason to be proud of the many famous singers their country has produced—Joe Nammon, Nellie Mairlper, Peer Torzen, Joan

Sullon and, above all, the glorious Dorimy Fasola Teedo, whose name will forever be graven on the hearts of all true Strines. Madame Teedo—known to all her adorers as the Mordialloc Magpie—is unique in Strine musical history. Her golden voice and tempestuous personality are indeed legendary, but it is as a lyricist and composer that her true brilliance is revealed. Perhaps the best-loved of her perennially popular songs are 'There Are Ferries at the Bomb of My Garden' and 'Dicey, Dicey, Give Me Your Ant, Sir, Do!' Another favourite, 'La, Fizzer Mannie's Planet—Think', has been translated into fifty-three languages. Even in the most remote parts of Norn Tare Tree and Vitamin Bay one may hear the natives singing, in their quaint accents, the well-known words of this moving ballad, which has here been translated as 'Love is Money Splattered Thick'.

Temps: *see* Harps.

Term Night Sear: Terminates here. (*See also* Rye-Wye.)

Terror Souse: One of a number of conjoined double or triple-storeyed dwellings found in older parts of some capital cities (Fissroy, Paddo, North Air Delight, etc.). Antonym: Gloria Soame (*q.v.*).

> We have bought ourselves a terror souse in Paddo
> In a district which is squalid but admired.
> It's a pity that the rooms are full of shadow,
> And the bathroom leaves so much to be desired.
>
> Of course we had to spend a bit of money;
> The plumbing was, well—you know, rather quaint.
> We live mostly in the kitchen where it's sunny.
> (It's wonderful what you can do with paint.)
>
> Our neighbours are artistic and they love us.
> (The ironwork, though meagre, is a dream.)

Mr Terego!
Dint note was
ute first.
Dint
U. U. Steffer
beard?
I thaw
chetterlong
beard

Essa Dibbet
me wife
sediwer
skettin twold
twearer beard.
Shiss edit mimey
look lichen
Noel
office boy

A 'thing' lives in the attic up above us.
We haven't seen it yet—just heard it scream.

Tiger: Imperative mood of the verb to take. As in: 'Tiger look at this, Reg, you wooden reader battit,' or 'Tiger perrer spargly guys.'

Titch, Gloria Sarah: Madame Titch is perhaps even more revered than Ned Kelly or the bellicose but lovable War Sigma Tilda. Gloria Sarah Titch has always been a great favourite of Strine elder statesmen, who often refer to her in their more exuberant exhortations, e.g. 'This is our Gloria Sarah Titch—we must defend it with your last drop of blood!' or 'If you vote for those dingoes you'll be betraying our Gloria Sarah Titch.'

To Gorf: To leave suddenly; to begin flying. As in: 'He to gorf like a rocket'; 'He to gorf like a batter to hell.' Antonym: To lairnd. As in: 'He to gorf at tempest four, Annie lairnded a Tairsenden atterbat harps nine.'

Trine: *see* Rye-Wye.

Uppendan: To and fro; backwards and forwards. As in: 'She walked uppendan Flinner Street farairs, an then she finey got a cabbome to Cannerbry.'

Utter Martyr: *see* Semmitch.

Wairtsed: *see* Jareedna.

Weird: Electric railway station near Hunner Street, Sinny. Trines leave Weird for Naw Sinny, Slennets and the Naw Shaw. (*See also* Naw Shaw; and Rye-Wye.) Note: Weird should not be confused with the English word *weird*, as in *They're a Weird Mob*.

Wezzme: Where is my. As in: 'Wezzme hembairg and wezzme earni-

But hula calf
trim
Y. limer Y?
Summon scotter look
calf trim.
Summer nester
Phillip E. Sworter
and gimmies
tier nawl

Nair
dent-shoe worry.
Iler calf trim.
Sleece tiger do.
Watsy effris tea?
Dar sneff
March dussy?
Undersea
effny think frizz
breckfuss?

form?' or 'Wezzme pressure-pack sherry and meem rangs an me autographed photo of Lassie?'

Wisperoo Des: A noted name in Strine literature. Notorious for his harshness, hated by the prisoners, feared by man and animal alike, Wisperoo Des is the brutal main character in the long epic poem 'Chris and Des', by Adam Lizzie Gorn. The following oft-quoted passage is from the famous duel scene in Act IV:

(Enter: Ned Kelly, carrying easel, brushes and several 44-gallon drums of synthetic enamel. Offstage, sounds of critics clicking ballpoint pens.)
　　Kelly: Harsh, harsh Wisperoo Des
　　And Chrissofer Robin have fallen danstairs.
　　Anorlerking sauces anorlerking smen
　　Are watching the mares and the birdies again.

Would never: Do not have. As in: 'You would never light wood germite?' or 'Ar would never glue.'

X: The twenty-fourth letter of the Strine alphabet; also plural of egg; also a tool for chopping wood.

Yeggowan: Do you intend travelling to? As in: 'Yeggowan Rare Wick Sairdy?' or 'Yeggowan E. Smelpen on Wensdy? Ora yeggowan togota Sunkilta?'

Zarf Trawl: Because after all. As in: 'Zarf trawl Leica nony doomy Bess.' Or: 'Zarf trawl wee rony flesh and blood wennit Saul boiled down.'

NOSE TONE UNTURNED

NOSE TONE UNTURNED

PEOPLE;
PREDICAMENTS;
POEMS;
BY

Afferbeck Lauder

Professor of Strine Studies,
University of Sinny

Illustrated by *Al Terego*

Contents

Acknowledgments

The author expresses his grateful acknowledgments to the *Sydney Morning Herald*, in which much of the material in this book originally appeared. He also expresses his gratitude to the many hundreds of correspondents who have so kindly offered him advice and information about obscure Strine words and phrases. He regrets that he has been unable to answer all these letters individually, and takes this opportunity of saying—Thank you.

He would also like to express his warmest thanks to the following people for their help in a variety of ways:

To A. T. B. for his continued invaluable criticism and advice;

To Judy Burns for permission to reproduce the music she wrote for Tim Pannelli's song;

To his assistant, Andrew Paragon, for his never-failing tolerance and patience;

To his secretary, Philippa Nibbly, for bringing, to page 104, only one of those sandwiches; and also for chair kinny spairlin;

And, finally, to Alistair Morrison, without whose help this book would never have been completed.

Foreword

I met Afferbeck Lauder for the first time many years ago, when he was staying in the house with my family. Then, of course, I didn't know his name—this was to be a fairly recent discovery. He was always, though you may now find this almost incredible, a shy, retiring sort of fellow. Brilliant, of course—at least I always found him so, and with a keen ear for the nuances of the language, I enjoyed his company more than most people's, and I certainly laughed at his wit more than at anyone else's. We were inseparable companions, and so I came to know him extraordinarily intimately; indeed he became almost a sort of alter ego. For some reason he always shunned the public gaze. He even went so far as to adopt various disguises from time to time, which gave us both a great deal of wry amusement. It was only after the publication of *Let Stalk Strine* that I was able to prevail upon him to come out into the open to accept his mantle of fame.

This new publication, which has given me enormous pleasure, brings you a more complete picture of the man than his previous work, crammed as it was with hard facts, could possibly have done. I hope you all enjoy it even half as much as I have.

Alistair Morrison
Sydney, 1966

A Day at the Big Store

He who enters shop with lady or davvy zed-red—Strine proverb

When I entered Suite 307 on the third floor of the Hotel Magna I was only mildly dismayed and not really at all surprised to find a rather patient-looking gorilla poring over some papers at the desk, and a large albino aardvark sitting on the bed, wearing an ill-fitting yellow wig, and sawing the tips off her claws—or perhaps she was painting her nails; I couldn't be sure which. It had, after all, been a morning of one extraordinary incident after another, and by now I was almost completely unflabbergastable.

What had happened was that, earlier, as I was walking to the bus, I had encountered a small boy on a surfskate—or rather he had encountered me. He had zoomed past me downhill on his way to the gum-vending machine, and had joggled me and screeched *'Ny'anng!'* into my good ear, giving me such a fright that I had jumped about two feet into the sky and had dropped my bifocals irretrievably down a stormwater grating. Since then I had, in my half blind state, been involved in a series of most disconcerting confrontations. I had raised my hat in polite greeting to a neighbour, and had said, 'Good morning, Mrs Kratchnoff. How are you, and how's Ron? How did the budgies like the kelp?' and had been shocked by her deep bass reply: 'Listen, mate, knock it off will you or I'll call the troopers.' The bus conductor had refused my fare because he was in fact a fireman, and the hairless and pitifully shrunken old woman to whom I gave my seat had waved a black snake at me and said, 'Goo!' several times before I discovered that she was a toddler with a licorice strap. And so it had continued the whole morning. How could I now be worried by such small-time stuff as a poring gorilla and a sawing aardvark?

The gorilla got up from the desk and shook my hand, 'Ah, Afferbeck. Nice to see you.' The aardvark stopped hacking her extremities, and smirked at me and said, 'Smf!' and I knew then that I was in the right room. It was clear now that the gorilla was not only human but was also my old friend Dr Willi Schkrambl of the Polyglot Institute at Grinzing. The aardvark was of course Madame Schkrambl. I'd made no mistake about the wig, though—it *was* a wig; her usual ill-fitting yellow one, through which she now ran her fingers, shaking her head back with a typically masculine flourish.

Dr Schkrambl, an anthropologist of considerable renown, had come to Australia to study some of the more obscure customs of the inhabitants, and to investigate and to record for his institute the intricate subtleties of the Strine language. Naturally I had offered to help in any way I could, and so here I was, for the twentieth day in succession, escorting him and his aardvark wife on a tour of local oddities. I had thought, when I first offered my services, that the whole operation would be a pushover, but I hadn't taken into account Madame Schkrambl's extraordinary energy and perseverance. She was indefatigable—I am not. My spirit is willing but my feet are weak.

I apologised for being late. After the usual shuffling around and talking about the weather Madame Schkrambl made it clear to me, by means of eye-rolling, sign language and what she thought was English, that we were today going on a tour of department stores. 'Oh no! Not that!' I heard my feet say. Her husband said he thought it would be a good opportunity to hear some specialised Strine. I don't think really that he had any part in the decision, but he always put on a convincing show of strength.

'Yuiff snar. Gsengel—so!' said Madame Schkrambl. As usual I didn't know what she was talking about but I could see, even in my monofocal, presbyopic condition, that she was hopping with restlessness, so, without further discussion, we took off.

'...dress material spiper pairten slidy snitwear all kiddieswear corsetry cropperdy travel good slidy sarnderwear maternity boutique and souvenirs goer *nar* please!' said the lift driver.

'Pliz klu—slom!' said Madame Schkrambl as we emerged onto the field of battle. She pointed a trembling finger at a sign which read: Budgetwear for the Mature Figure. Her eyes rolled with excitement, and her nostrils dilated so that she looked like a rocking mare. 'Pliz translite,' she said with husky joy.

'It says: Expensive clothes for fat old women,' I told her, but already she was in a semi-trance.

'Lesker datter this quick,' said Dr Schkrambl, justifiably panic-stricken, but determined, as usual, to speak Strine whenever possible. 'Lesker danter the tool snardware,' he continued. 'Ah wanner gessem Sam Piper 'n' turps.' But he was too late—much too late; Madame Schkrambl was already almost out of eyeshot, burrowing into the budget wear with a saleswoman who had appeared, like a bush fly, suddenly from nowhere.

Dr Schkrambl tried again. 'Gretlklein, lesker datter this, *dear*...' he shouted, his cupped hands to his mouth. But it was hopeless. We looked at each other. 'About an hour, I would think, wouldn't you?' I said.

'Yair, batter narret least,' he answered with resignation. 'Or nairer nar feven. Ware, lesket bacter work. You ready?' He sat down on the floor with his back against a display of drastically reduced imported famous-name knitwear oddments many below cost, and motioned to me to sit down beside him. He took out a notebook and pencil, and fingered his way down the pages.

'Yair, seewee are,' he said. 'Hisswear we leftorf at the concert la snite. Now—what's the English for: I rare jaw la spook—reel good. Air nephew ritter nennie moorpook slightly?'

'In English,' I told him, 'you'd say: I read your last book and found it quite entertaining. And do you expect to have anything new published in the near future?' He noted all this down carefully.

'Now, bairns?' he asked. 'Bairns are what you call kiddies, I suppose? Same as in Scotland.'

'Oh no,' I corrected him. 'Bairns are either musical groups—you know like chairs bairns—or else they can be—ah, sort of loops, like rubber bairns. You remember the line: The mussel zonny sprawny arm stuttairt li-gine bairns.'

'I see, I see. Well now…' he consulted his notebook. 'What about Hazzy? This means: Has he?'

'No, hazzy means: How is he? As in: Hazzy gairt nonnets cool? Or: Hazzy gairt non wither mare thorgon?'

'Ah, good. Now, what's machewer mean?'

'Machoor,' I corrected his pronunciation. 'Machoor means: ripe; fully developed; experienced. For example, you'd say: Listen, chicken, what mortgage you want thanner machoor manner the world like me? Although, strictly speaking, when you address a lady as chicken, it is more correct to say machoor rooster of the world.'

'Ah, so! Machoor rooster. Reel good.' He made copious notes. I remembered that he had always taken a keen interest in birds, and was in fact president of the Grinzing branch of Voluptuaries Anonymous.

'So!' He nodded his head several times with satisfaction. 'And now,' he continued, 'here's one which has puzzled me. What's Dopey's prize? A consolation prize, perhaps?'

'Oh no, Dopey's prize is a sort of warning, as in: Okay, go ahead and bitey zearoff, but dopey's prize diffy bite spak; arf trawly zony human.'

'Ah, good, good. Well now, what's a knotter fiker?'

I peered at the budgetwear to see what was going on. They were apparently still engaged in the preliminaries; not even at the trying-on stage yet. I was getting hungry. I had a headache from the effort of surviving in a hostile environment without bifocals. I knew that before the day was over we would have walked through miles of department store, and that I would be suffering the agonies of British Museum feet. I forced myself to attend to what my companion had been saying.

'Knotter fiker?' I said. 'Well, that's incomplete really. It is usually followed by some such word as nairlpit. For instance, you'd say—or I would, anyway, that's for sure: We woker meara gain. Knotter fiker nairlpit.'

In the distance I could see Madame Schkrambl and the bush fly lady disappearing into the trying-on rooms, each carrying about a dozen multicoloured machoor figure jobs. Dr Schkrambl sighed patiently. He shut his notebook and put it back in his pocket. 'Ware lider nair bare chew,' he said, 'but I mungry. Hair batter cabbage Eno—Anna bitter G. Skite?' He spoke Strine like a native—a remarkable achievement.

Hagger Nigh Tell?

Hagger nigh telephime reely reel?
Hadder Y. Noah Fimere?
Car sigh ony nowered I thing ky feel,
An maybe I'm knotty veneer.

I mipey no lesson I mipey no more
Than a shadder we idle fancy.
Prabzyme the moon! Can I Telfer Shaw
That I'm nodgers a nant named Nancy?

I coobie jar sreely a loafer bread,
Or a horse, or a bird called Gloria.
I mipey alive—but I coobie dead,
Or a phantasmabloodygoria.

Hagger nigh tellime notonia dream,
Cook tarpner mare chick's pell?
Cor sigh my pig zackly what I seem,
Bar towg nigh *reely* tell?

. . .

Wunker nawlwye stell; yegger nawlwye snow
If you're reelor yerony dreaming;
Yellopoff the topoff your nirra stow,
A new wafer the sander the screaming.

The Gentlest Man

I arrived at the airport with time to spare. It was cold, and I stood near one of the heaters while I waited for the big jet to arrive.

I took out Geoffrey's letter and read it again. He would be in Australia for a few days, he had written, before going on to Melbourne (typical), and he was looking forward to seeing me. He was preparing a paper on semantics, which he was to read to some egghead show or other he'd been made a fellow of. And what did I think of the title? 'Mystery Lingo Bid Baffles Euroglots'. He wanted to include some examples of Strine and other obscure (!) languages. He had heard of my appointment to the post of Professor of Strine Studies at the University of Sinny, and could I give him an hour or so on such and such a date? And he was mine sincerely, Geoffrey.

Obscure indeed! How like him. Anything he didn't know much about was obscure. He probably even thought Australia was an English-speaking country; he was incredibly ignorant. Still, he was a nice fellow, kind and gentle.

I looked at my watch. The plane was late. I wandered over to the newsstand and looked at the near-naked girls on the magazine covers. Pretty girls they were, too. One, I noticed, a particularly robust type, proudly overtopping her skimpy bra, bore the legend *Two Big Liftouts*. My mind started to wander along a warm, familiar track, when suddenly—it happened!

Paaaaaaaaaahr! Graggle! Tzingggggg! Pikpik! An appalling noise, practically inside my head. I was standing immediately below one of the public address outlets.

This sort of thing is always happening to me. Just thinking about something, quietly minding my own business, and suddenly—Peng! Someone runs into me on a bicycle, or something blows up in my face.

James Bond never goes on like this; why do I? Absent-minded, I suppose. The absent-minded professor. James Bond! I wondered if Geoffrey was a spy. Perhaps he was really coming out here to ask me...

Poong! Grag grag! Aaaaaaa-pik! I jumped again, but only a few inches this time. *Yorred hessian plaize. Flight glargle glargle glar Baggokokko Sicker Paw nair riving ah-pem ah-pem ah-pem. Pik!* Well, here it was. I moved over to where the crowd had gathered, and waited for him to come through Customs.

I went forward with my hand out, to greet him, but he never saw me—just stared right through me, looking for someone. Me, I suppose. I had to grab his arm.

'Airfferbairk! My dear chairp!' He beamed at me with pleasure. 'Dewno I dint even nerr you.'

'I've had my hair cut shorter,' I said.

'No, no, old chairp. It's because you look sirmer cholder.'

He always was completely truthful; I can't imagine how he had managed to last so long on a newspaper. Still, he didn't have to be quite so brutal.

Eventually I got him settled into his hotel. We sat down in his suite and had tea and sandwiches. Then he took out a very small notebook and a silver pencil about the size of a match. He looked at me indulgently, a gentle smile on his happy, foolish face, and said, glancing at his very thin watch, 'Airps-loo-lair marfless to see you, old chairp. Now I've got about twenty minutes. Tell me airfrithing about Strine.'

Everything! Twenty minutes! After thirty years of research!

'Snow datter batcher, yerron yerrone,' I said, and watched him blink.

'What's that, old chairp?'

'Snore flotta effter tellion lesser narfer nair.'

He stopped smiling, and opened and shut his mouth a few times. 'Liss-nole chairp, do talk English.' He leant forward and patted my hand gently.

'Ah-na, Chair-free, jar slesky pon torgon Strine,' I said.

He put down his notebook and pencil. Then he got through to room service and ordered a bottle of scotch.

'Answer mice,' I said.

'And some ice,' he repeated. He didn't say anything more until we each had a drink in front of us. Then all he said was, 'Ah!'

'Tell me, Geoffrey,' I said. 'This work you're doing. Marspy ferry in a resting.' He just stared at me with his mouth open. The time had come to stop matter-mincing.

'Look, Geoffrey, don't you realise this is a foreign country? You can't talk English all the time as though you were in Dijon, or Gothenburg, or Zurich or somewhere. You're in Australia now, not Europe, and if you want to get anywhere you'll have to learn the language. And it'll certainly take you more than twenty minutes.'

'Yes, old chairp. I see that now. I hadn't realised. Vair good of you to make it so clear.' He was so subdued now that I felt sorry for him, and a little ashamed. After all, he was such a nice, gentle fellow, really.

'Now look, Geoff,' I said, 'we haven't got much time. So let's take a few simple phrases—the sort of thing you'll need to get you through the next few days. There won't be time for nice distinctions, and cosy, finical hoo-ha. Just the rough stuff. You mightn't like this way of learning a language, but, well, yell jess tefter get chews twit.'

He sat up straight. 'I'll have to get what?'

'Chews twit,' I repeated. 'Youlga chews twit!'

He started to smile. 'Chews twit. Yes, I see. Get chews twit. Arlga chews twit. How's that?' He waited anxiously for praise.

'Very good indeed,' I said. 'Excellent. Now what's this I'm holding up?'

'A plastic raincoat, of course.'

'No, try again.'

He moved his lips around, silently. I watched his silly face light up.

'A plair stig raim court?'

'No, no. Nottingham, perhaps. Or Dublin or somewhere. But not Strine. Pleh. Pleh…' I prompted him, coaxed him, and finally he got it.

'A plesty crine coat, a plesty crine coat, a plesty bloody crinecoat.' He was grinning now, and somehow looked harder, and tougher. He made an odd sort of movement, and for a moment I thought he was going to spit on the floor.

'Well now,' I continued, 'let's take a typical, everyday situation. The sort of thing that's bound to happen if you're going to be here for a few days. Yes, I know. Say you're travelling in a suburban train. A young man gets in and sits beside you. He pulls out a flick-knife and starts slashing at the upholstery. Now what do you do?'

'I'd say to him, Now look here, old chairp. No, that can't be right. No, I don't really know what I'd do. I give up; what should I say to the fellow?'

'Well, to begin with, you don't *say* anything. What you have to *do* is—now, are you ready? Wait for it—you kingie minner teeth!'

'I kingie minner teeth. I kingie minner teeth!' he shouted with delight. He punched his right fist into his left palm, and spat on the floor. 'I kingie minner teeth! I kingie minner teeth, inner teeth, inner teeth, TEETH!' He couldn't stop. He was jumping up and down, his face transformed. 'I kingie minner teeth! I kingie minner teeth agair, nanna, gair nanna, GAIRN!'

A little line of saliva ran down from one corner of his mouth. It was frightening. I was beginning to feel as a psychiatrist must feel when he has dug too deep, too quickly, and has hit something. I hoped I hadn't created a Frankenstrine monster.

I tried to calm him by talking English, but it didn't work.

'Take it easy,' I said. But perhaps he didn't understand English any more.

'Yuma sketcher cell farner control. Try talking English. You know—English?'

'Snow ewe smite,' he said. 'I've gedadda the wire-fit.' He had me really worried now. Would I have to give him largactil to terminate it? He was worried too, apparently, very worried.

'Arkahn's top! Warm-eye gonadoo? Hair my gona gedadda this?'

'Take it easy, Geoff. Take it easy.'

'Tiger teasie, tiger teasie. Saul-wright few!' He was in a panic now, giving little low moans, and kicking a pillow around the room, screaming, 'Kingie minner teeth, the drongo!' Then he started to cry. He picked up the Bible from the bedside table, and got down on his knees. 'Matthew, Ma, Kloogenjahn! Oh, parrot I slossed! Oh, Lord, mike me a pommagairn. I wonna go woam. I wommy mummy. I dough wonnerby star gear frevver.' He was wailing wildly and tearing at his forearms. There was no time now to get help. No time for doctors with needles. There was only one thing to do. I picked up the whisky bottle, and let him have it—right onny zoxyput!

I got him onto the bed, and covered him up with a blanket. He'd just have to sleep it off. I hoped he *would* sleep it off. I sat down and waited. No point in getting anyone else in, until I saw how he was when he came to. I'd have to be very careful not to speak anything but English. Someone else might easily say something like 'Prab zeiche nelpew,' and he'd be off again. I sat back and waited.

Gradually he began to look a little better; a little bit less like Jekyll and Hyde, and a bit more like his usual self—like Laurel and Hardy. About an hour later he stirred and opened his eyes. I waited anxiously for his first words. He sat up, very slowly.

'King…King…' he said. I reached for the bottle, but he lay down again. Then he sat up once more. 'King. King. I say, old chairp, I've had a very odd dream. Something about teeth. Very odd.' He looked puzzled. 'I say, old chairp, what happened?'

I was so relieved I nearly cried. Too relieved, really; I relaxed and, without thinking, said, 'You got star ginter the turp smite.' However, nothing happened; he just looked more puzzled than ever.

'I must have had a drop too much. Joy good of you to look after me, old chairp. What's happened to my head?'

'There it is. Look—on your neck. Take it out and put it under the tap for a while.'

He got up and had a shower, and in about half an hour he seemed perfectly all right, and was asking me about the Strine language, and could I give him an hour or so tomorrow? I said I'd have to check with my secretary.

He thanked me again for being so kind. He couldn't understand how it had happened. I explained that the scotch had been bottled in Australia, and so it was much stronger than anything he'd get at home. It seemed to satisfy him.

By the time I left he was whistling softly, and saying 'King king king' gently to himself. But then he does everything gently. The gentlest man I've ever known—I think.

The Bossa Nye

Ware niker tinter work now
The bossa zinner hedomy;
Ickisser smee, and sair, 'Swill yubie mine?'
I got a rillked lurk now;
'I lar few, dear,' he sedomy,
But ice air, 'Gee, it sneely ah-pa snine.'

. . .

I fleft me jobber twirk now;
The bosket spy withairt me;
A niken stayer tome a slardger slife.
I give a little smirk now;
The bossle torga bairt me:
'Me sekkertry has nowbie cummy wife.'

Big Deal with Miss Highwater

A few days ago I was sitting at my desk, in a semi-comatose condition, trying, without much success, to digest one of those meals for which the staff canteen is famous all over Australia and the South Pacific area. Spaghetti and baked beans on toast with mashed potatoes had been followed by something which on Mondays, Wednesdays and Fridays is known as Cabinet Pudding, and on Tuesdays and Thursdays as Spotted Dog. All this had been adequately irrigated with semi-opaque tea from a monolithic lolly-pink cup.

I remembered having been informed years ago, by an advertisement, that the acid in my stomach would burn a hole in the carpet. I now appreciated the undeniable truth of this majestic statement. I helped myself to still another spoonful of sodium bicarbonate from a jar which I keep suspended from the ceiling on a length of string, and called to my secretary in the next room.

'Miss Nibbly, kannewka minneara minute?' I find I nearly always speak Strine in moments of anguish or dismay.

Miss Nibbly came running, eyebrows raised.

'Air you all rate, professor? Orv you bin lenching et the centeen again?'

'Miss Nibbly,' I said, 'I have a premonition that something terrible is about to happen.' I looked down to see if any holes were appearing in the carpet yet.

She looked at her watch. 'York weight rate, professor. Miss Highwater is coming to do you et three.'

Suddenly it all came back to me, bringing with it a sinking feeling in the pit of what was once my stomach. Good heavens! Helen Highwater—and no place to hide.

This internationally famous journalist had telephoned earlier in the week to say that she would like to 'do' me in the weekly women's journal which she edits. Obviously she was hoping to increase her own apparent intellectual stature by having me appear in her lousy journal, but what could I do? I abhor the limelight, but I had to consider the interests of the university; after all, *Womb and Sty* has an enormous circulation. And so I had agreed. 'Don't forget to bring a photographer,' I had said.

And now she would be here any minute. I straightened my collar, brushed away a few traces of Spotted Dog, and started to look distinguished. I could hear an increasing commotion in the outer office. She had arrived.

'My dear Helen.' I rose and greeted her. 'How nice to see you.'

This was not, strictly speaking, true; it wasn't nice to see her at all. She is a noisy, over-emphatic woman in her late fifties. She was wearing, as usual, a face such as one ordinarily wouldn't expect to see outside a zoo.

'Afferbeck, dear boy,' she trumpeted, 'how are you?' Involuntarily, I glanced up to see if the mahout was there, sitting on her head.

'Not bad, Helen…' I started to tell her about my indigestion, hoping to follow up with details of recent visits from various viruses. Then I planned to touch lightly on the more popular, semi-chronic items like slipped disc and insomnia. But I could see that she was fidgeting, and had disconnected her hearing aid. This is what is so maddening about the woman—asks you a question, and then doesn't listen to the answer.

She had settled herself in a chair and was scratching around in a large handbag, from which she now extracted a notebook the size of a ledger. She reconnected her hearing aid and lit a cigarette. I cleared my throat.

'Well,' I said, 'I assume that your readers will want to know all the usual things. My background and qualifications, and so on. Then, I suppose, a few comments about my next book, my plans for the future.

Perhaps a few paragraphs about my philosophy of life. A brisk run through the wife and kiddies, and how I first became interested in the Strine language. That should about cover it, don't you think?'

'Of course, dear boy,' she replied. 'But there's a little matter I'd like to discuss with you first.' She tore two or three pages out of the ledger, folded them in half, and sat on them. 'As you know,' she went on, 'I've just returned from a journey all over Australia by bicycle. Well, of course, I met and talked with all kinds of people. Desert tribesmen, housewives, truckies, bush nurses, doggers, hatters, shearers, swaggies, opal miners, rabbiters, lurk men, lubras, and doctors—both flying and witch.' She paused, and smiled her crinkly, moon-faced smile.

'I thought of you, dear boy,' she went on. 'And I collected for you a dozen or more quite rare Strine words and phrases. I'm sure most of them will be new to you.'

So that's how the old bag got those billiard-table legs—pedalling about the hinterland on a two-wheeler. Still, it was good of her to think of my interests in this way.

'That's extraordinarily kind of you, Helen,' I said, leaning across and patting what I thought was probably a knee. I held out my hand for the loot.

'Just a moment, dear boy,' she said. 'These are valuable.' I didn't catch on at first. Then, suddenly, I saw what she meant. The old camel wanted to *sell* them to me. I was horrified. I stalled for time. I went over to the window and swatted a few dreamy blowflies. I bit a few finger-nails. I got out the polish and started to clean my shoes. I mustn't seem too anxious. I went back slowly, and sat down again.

'You must be joking, of course, Helen. But then you always were a remarkably witty woman.'

'I said they're valuable,' she repeated. She was now clutching the pages in her mighty fist.

What could I do? I had to have them, but I couldn't let her know this. What was my next move to be? I couldn't just say—How much?

'How much?' I said.

'Fifty dollars a word,' she replied, without hesitation.

'You're mad, you hideous old dragon!' I shouted at her with icy dignity, dancing up and down.

'First of all, dear boy, don't call me old. And secondly, if you don't want them I'll let the Rockefeller Foundation have them; they've already made me an offer.'

Good heavens! This was appalling. I'd be the laughing stock of the academic world if anyone published them before I did—this was my subject. She was probably bluffing, but I couldn't take any risks. I must remain quite calm. I banged on the desk with both fists, as imperturbable as ever.

'Listen to me, you fiendish old trombone,' I screeched at her. 'Where do you think I'm going to get that sort of money? I'll give you twenty dollars each. How many are there?'

'Oooo—about a dozen or so. No, dear boy, not a cent less than fifty dollars.'

A dozen! At fifty dollars! I called out to my assistant, Dr Paragon, and asked him to work it out for me. I finished polishing my shoes while I waited.

Eventually, slide rule in hand, he came in with the answer—seven hundred and forty seven dollars!

'Seffer narnet and voice airven.' I broke into Strine in my anguish. 'Why couldn't you have left me alone with my stomach, you web-footed old bat? I was happy before you came. And how do I know you're not conning me? You old slug; you ought to be pole-axed. How about a free sample?'

'Okay,' she agreed, after some hesitation, 'one free sample with translation, and two without.' She peered down at the pages, 'Soym Gwynn,' she said at last. 'Soym Gwynn. That's a very rare one. I got it from a pearl diver up near Broome. Cost me a packet, too. He was telling me about the time his First Engineer was drowned in the Coral

Sea. I soym gwynn, he said to me, butter dinsim carmairt. Northern Strine, very valuable.' She smiled happily as she ran a horny finger down the page, looking for goodies.

'And how about these?' she went on. 'Arlu clugger, and dokey ponner. I tell you, dear boy, you're getting them cheap. And here's a song about Y. Lezzer Kahn. Oooo, and at least a dozen more, accurately translated and copiously annotated.'

I was shaking with excitement. What could an arlu clugger be? Who was Y. Lezzer Kahn, that they should have felt impelled to write a song about him? What was a dokey ponner—animal, vegetable or mineral?

'Forty dollars?' I said. But I knew it was a waste of time; my trembling hands gave me away.

'Listen, dear boy, I said fifty—and I meant it. Now hurry, I mustn't be late for the Prime Minister.'

I reached for my chequebook. My capitulation was complete.

'How do you spell your name, Helen? With one scream or two?' I made out the cheque for a hundred and fifty dollars, and borrowed the rest from petty cash.

She handed me the pages. I went out with her and helped her onto her bicycle, and pushed her off down the hill. I ran back to my office, sick with excitement. Arlu clugger! Y. Lezzer Whatsisname! I rubbed my sweating hands with joy.

I locked the door, and opened up my prize. Nice, neat handwriting, too. Good old Helen, always so reliable.

Dokey ponner (I read): meaning, Please stop reminding me. As in: Okay, okay, I said I was sorry. Jars dokey ponner battered. Source: A psychiatrist at Lightning Ridge, scolded by his wife for having put largactil in her lolly-water.

Arlu clugger: I resemble. As in: Arno arlu clugger nairedale, buttem rilly a border collie. Source: A sheep dog called Caliban, at Peak Hill, New South Wales.

Pidiot Stoo: It is unfortunate that it is too… As in: Pidiot stoo early flunch. Canniver bitter bren jairm? Source: A ten-year-old hyperthyroid bread-and-jam addict, son of a Rockhampton cane-cutter.

Y. Lezzer Kahn: Character in the song 'The Law Y. Spear Ningland Y. Lezzer Kahn Treeline'. Source: The occasion of an evening party after the picnic races at Gooblawookla, near Eucla. We all sat around the campfire, and sang all the old favourites, 'The Law Y. Spear Ningland', 'Long Wider Tier Prairie' and 'Arse Wheat Miss Drear Flife'.

I ran my eyes over the lovely lovely list. Thaw ninny side; Fordyce and Fawnite Sweek; noker parison; umpziggen tardafit; Theng Q. Bubbeye; Karkasova chicken; how swarming; the Serviette Union; far spola; Hymen Island; snow trarpler tall; ease dregs; gun cedar woofer the trees; Noah to park; the dotted lion; welker mome; wee jar stono; mife yon say; sloombar…

And about a dozen more. I'd certainly got my money's worth. Perhaps she'd given me some of the Prime Minister's too, by mistake. What a bargain! Only seven hundred and something dollars. Why, they'd have cost me twice that on the black market. Good old Helen. An attractive woman too, in a repellent sort of way.

La Dolce Vita

I think that I shall never see
A treer sluffly yazzer poem.
The cool fresh water snoffer me,
But champagne by the jeroboam.

I got no time for lousy trees,
Withaw lem leaves an birds an nests;
The darling starling isstomy
The dreariest of lousy pests.

Gimme the brighter sneon lights;
The laugh teroff the dancing girls,
With mini-skirts an lacy tights,
An stardust in their lacquered curls.

Gimme a car with plennier power,
An gimmier drinker tenny cost.
This is my finest, final hour;
I mitching to be level-crossed.

Bra Sharp Your Strine

Calm nodomy a gine, but cider Airthens,
Timer nath mighty zephyr-lasting mention
A ponner beached verger the salt flar,
Do once a die withis embossed froth
The turbulent surchall carver; thither Carmen,
Lep-mye grive's tone be or Rorricle:
Lips, lets air word skobyen, Lang gwichairnd:
Wadders a miss, Ply gannon Fection mairnd.
Grive zony bee-men's work, san Death air gine;
Saar, nide thy beams, Timer nath dunny's Rhine.

Few occupations are more rewarding, more deeply satisfying, than translating Shakespeare into Strine. I had already completed *Hairmlet* and *A Winner Style*, and now, at last, here I was almost at the end of *Time Honour Vairthens*. I would have given anything to be able, now, to start on *Macbeth*. Of course I still had a few senatorial loose ends to clear up with Timon; Alcibiades and the epitaph and everything. But these could wait; Macbeth was calling me, clamouring to be done into Strine—the noblest language of them all. But more pressing things were at hand. Reluctantly I put Timon aside; with a sigh I dismissed Macbeth. It was time for the half-yearly examination of the second-year students. I called Miss Nibbly and asked her to give me the final draft of the paper I had prepared.

I read it through carefully. Not bad—not bad at all, really. I had thought that I would need to do some more work on it, but no, it seemed okay. Comprehensive, varied, not too difficult and yet not too obviously a pushover. I decided to let it go as it was. I corrected the spelling of the word *earmile,* and asked Miss Nibbly to run off the usual number of copies. Then I locked the door and drew the curtains. I took down *Macbeth.* At last, at last! Meanwhile, Miss Nibbly was hard at work.

STRINE II—Half-yearly Examination (Possible marks: 100)

(1) Who are Arch and T. Nairns? Where are Lucas Heights and Fagger's Heights? What is the meaning of: A Skymer Snairk Ellie? (5 marks)

(2) Translate the following into English: She scone orphan tyken the kiddie swither; He nair fradder penny Toohey snime; Chew plonker the bowling clarp? (5 marks)

(3) Write twenty-five words in Strine about any three of the following: Phenobarbecuticle; Leprecapricornucopia; Earmile and Surfer Smile; The Flying Sorceress of Bonnie Doom. (5 marks)

(4) Compose a telegram of seventy to a hundred words, and include as many as possible of the following Strine words: Ice-cream; flake; dim; choir; Carmen; cauliflowers; doubt; crairnonnie; try; low; sawn-off; butcher; dough; rand; loafer; sighed; sneck; eyesore; craw; dadda; zed; sore; lassie.

The following is given as an example of the sort of thing that is required. However you are expected to use your own imagination, and not merely to copy or rearrange.

    EYESORE A BIG DOG CARMEN AWARDS ME IT WAS
    A CAULI FLOWERS WERE A RAND E SNECK ANDY
    WORE A CRAIRNONNIE ZED GOLLY ITSA CAULI
    ICE-HEAD IT LOOKS LIKE SAWN-OFF LASSIE

OR RIN TIN TINNERS CHOIR I PADDER DIM ON THE CROWN BUT HE LOOKED CRAW SIGHED AT ME AND SAID DOUGH BUTCHER RAND SORE LOAFER ME MISTER ICE-CREAM DADDA DIM OOOOOOOOO I GOT SUCH A FRIGHT I FLAKE TRY DOUBT—AFFERBECK LAUDER. (20 marks)

(5) Translate the following into English:

You mask etcher hair cut, dear; Yuma sketcher rare cut, dear; U. Masker chaw rare cart, dear; Yelljer steffter gair chair cart, dear; Well lacquer dyno your a spaulder snegg? You never take your Turbanoff—dear. (10 marks)

(6) Translate the following into Strine:

Did you know your left foot's missing?

Why, so it is. I wonder when that happened.

Isn't it painful?

Well, now that you mention it, I have been screaming a lot lately.

Just shows you, doesn't it?

Well, since you put it that way, I suppose it does. (10 marks)

(7) What, if anything, do you find improbable about the following?

He kissed her tenderly. 'Darling, your skin is like spung gold, and your hair like a Pharaoh's pedal. Dearest, you are Soap Rashes Toomey. I la few; arl nair fletchoo go.' With grater motion he crushed a rinny zarms. Then he put on his glasses, and looked at her more closely. He drew back in dismay. 'It's the wife. Crikey!' He kissed her once more, not quite so tenderly, saying, 'Look, fellas. No hands!' (5 marks)

(8) Write out in full the words of either of the following Strine songs:
(a) Ammonia vagabond lava, or (b) Ammonia burden a gilded cage. (10 marks)

(9) Who wrote the following? Translate into Strine:

'Dear Oedipus,' Jocasta said,
'Be jovial and jocose.
Let Mum take the worry
Out of being close.' (5 marks)

(10) Translate the following story into Strine, but first fill in the blanks, using any of the material appended:

It was midnight at Limehouse, and a quick brown fog jumped over the lazy docks. Snow White heard the sound of breaking glass echoing through the empty house. She heard the shot, and the muffled scream— then silence. She was trapped. 'Waddle-eye do?' she whispered, 'The secret sleek tout!' Slowly, the door opened, and .... appeared in the doorway. Even in the half-light she could see the blood on his gloved hands, and the .... which he carried so nonchalantly. Suddenly .... appeared beside him, carrying .... 'Turner rand!' he barked. 'Wait!' He laughed cruelly. He took something from the pocket of his trench coat, and threw it at her feet. It was ....

Now select those of the following items which you think would be most appropriate, and fill in the blanks above:

An ear; a bag of manure from a well-rotted cow; a facsimile of 'The Blue Door', gift-wrapped, and bearing a card with the words 'Good luck, Reg. Get well soon. All the best from your workmates at the sweatshop'; a rattle-waving baby boy dressed in pink; three half-inch Whitworth spanners; a diving helmet, complete with smiling head; three witchetty grubs in an elastic band; a cube of very canned pineapple; the Loch Ness Monster as Hamlet; two quandongs; a small bunch of tansy; something rather nasty-looking which she couldn't identify in the half-light, but which looked sticky, and had beady little eyes; two pairs of Grace Wade shoes; an Irish terrier with his mouth full of carrageen; the man who broke the Bank of Monte Carlo's auntie—I mean the one with twelve fingers who suffered intermittently from herpes—the auntie, I mean, not the fingers; a left foot, tattooed with the word 'Mother'; Little Dorrit with a hole in her forrit; three more diving helmets; and the other foot. (20 marks)

(11) Complete the following Strine poem, and name the author:

I musker dauta the CSR, Ken,
So tie my ship tour buoy.
A norlye ask is a gallon cask
Of overproof cocky's joy. (5 marks)

The Postman's Whistle

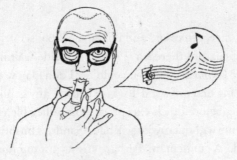

I dreamed I heard the postman's whistle
Whistle like a scream,
I found, to my surprise, that his'll
Whistle like my dream.

The next day, at the Embassy,
I met Professor Lauder,
And heard him, to a member, say,
'Miss Gem, a poyna forda!'

That night I tried to dream in Strine,
And dream in Strine I did.
My dreams in Strine, I find, are fine;
I dreamed a mazzer kid.

. . .

I dremm diurda postie swizzle
Wizzle liger scream.
Annizzle rogg-yer; E. sair zizzle
Wizzle like my dream.

The Case of the Missing Torso

'Skew smee, professor,' said Philippa Nibbly, scratching her ear with a pencil, 'but there's a gentleman atside waiting to see you.' A gentleman? I wondered who it could be; I don't know any gentlemen. I glanced at my diary to see if I was expecting any gentleman, but there was nothing before lunch except an almost illegible entry, apparently written by me without my knowledge, 'Sandra's birthday lemons check brake fluid.' A gentleman? Perhaps it was just another professor, and not a gentleman at all. Or perhaps it was someone from Hollywood, wanting to make a film about me. I wondered what they had in mind for the title: *The Hero of Dare Nunda*, perhaps, or *Lauder the Flies*. Or even *Birth of a Notion*. After all…

Miss Nibbly broke in on my dreams. 'I think he's a policeman,' she said, uneasily. 'He looks like a policeman.' Good lord, what had I done? I tried to recall if I had been in any hit-run incidents recently, or armed robberies. Had I concealed any torsos under the floorboards of the Department? I was relieved to find that my record, if not actually spotless, was—well, clean enough. As far as I could remember I hadn't even bashed anyone lately. I checked my pulse. It was almost back to normal. I came out from under the desk and sat in my chair again. 'Oh, police?' I said casually. 'Really? Ask him to come in.'

As he entered the room I could see at a glance that he was a policeman. A high-up one too; he had it written all over him. A big man, he looked competent and hard, and he had an unmistakable air of authority. Probably Assistant Commissioner. But why did he want to see *me*?

Whatever it was I would need to handle the situation very carefully, very tactfully. It would be best to treat the whole thing casually—with the lightheartedness of the innocent.

'Good morning, Assistant Commissioner. Ugh! Agh! Ooooooo—

Ugh!' I had inadvertently shut my left little finger inside the desk drawer. I lit a pencil with a cigarette. 'And what can we do for you?' I asked him. 'No torsos under this floor, I'm afraid. Sorry to disappoint you. Ha ha ha.' I deftly extracted what was left of my little finger from the drawer. I stubbed out my pencil on the calendar, and offered him the diary: 'Smoke?' I wondered idly how I would feel if he did find a torso under the floor, or even a couple of legs in a cupboard somewhere. There was a long and ominous silence. He stared at me open-mouthed and apparently alarmed.

'I muspy go anatomy mind,' he said. 'Yuper Fessor Lauder? Arno! I muspy inner wrong room, or I muspy gohen ranner bairnd.'

'No, no, Commissioner?' I promoted him—just to be on the safe side. 'You're in the right room. But there are no legs or anything like that here. No loot even. Nothing. Ha ha…ha…'

'Look, perfessor,' he said. 'Muspy summer stike.' He handed me a card. Hoomit, Maik & Surne Pty Ltd, I read, Market Research, Mass Communications Review and Counsel, Statistical Analysis, Public Opinion and Relationship Bureau, Business and Management Consultants, Ogden Hoomit, Director. It was a big card, it had to be; but then, he was a big man.

Really, I thought, I'll have to do something about Miss Nibbly— have to give her a good talking to. All this scare about police. Making a fool of me in front of strangers. Why, anyone could see at a glance that this was no policeman. Here was a serious student of mass communications and all that other stuff. A dedicated research worker like myself—a fellow scientist; he had it written all over him.

'My dear Mr Hoomit,' I said, 'I'm delighted to meet you at last. We've heard all about you of course, and the wonderful work you're doing down there at—I glanced at his card—at H. M. & S. Wonderful! Don't mind my little jokes about torsos; I mistook you for someone else. You look very much alike—almost identical, in fact, except that she's much smaller and walks with a limp. Breeds poodles, too—nice little woman. Do you know her?' I didn't know how to stop now. I offered him another cigarette. 'Miniatures,' I said. 'Poodles, I mean—not cigarettes; it's a king-size. Tell me more about this research now. Must be fascinating.'

He was staring at me again. He came to with a start as I pushed the cigarette into his open mouth and held a light in front of it. 'Kink's eyes? Poodles?' he said, not taking his eyes from me. 'What poodles?'

'Well, this girl I was telling you about. The one who looks so like you, I mean. You know—the one that limps? Well, these poodles of hers—the miniatures…' I stopped. This wasn't getting us anywhere. I couldn't afford to spend the whole morning talking about poodles to a complete stranger. Who did he think I was? It was ridiculous. I was a busy man, with a full programme ahead of me—Sandra's birthday and the lemons and everything.

'Look, let's start again,' I said. 'Tell me why you're here, and I'll tell you all about the poodles later—if we have time.'

He shrugged his shoulders, and shook his head in a dazed fashion. He took a drag at his cigarette. Gradually he seemed to collect his wits. He opened up an impressive-looking black leather case with an inbuilt filing system.

'Nowper fessor,' he started off, 'I wunner a fewpie good enough to answer a few questions. My commany spinker missioned by the mannerfecturers of (he named a well-known detergent) twassertain the exac percentage…'

I found my attention wandering swiftly. What the hell was all this about? '…Now we fine television viewers have, like yourself, bin moce quoprative. We finer fwee reely analyse the situation weaken put moce viewers innu one of at least fork adder grease. Now weraz the morgan serftif viewer may have certain predgersez, the morse fister-kited viewer, like your good self, will, on the other hand, be even mork worpative. Nowf we drawper graph—like so…' He had produced a pad of graph paper, and was now setting up a small adding machine on my desk. The situation was getting out of hand; we'd have been better off with the poodles. He talked incessantly while he worked at the graph. He made rapid calculations on the adding machine, and plotted in the figures of a spectacular curve.

'Core satsoni to give you a rah fidea of howt workzout, anna corsin ackshell practice, as I thing kule red leer gree, it soma cheesier…'

'Look, Mr Hoomit, I must tell you about these poodles.' I tried hard to regain control, but he just waved his left hand in my face in a tictac gesture, and raised his voice. 'Nowper fessor, jumine telling meek zackly what your considered opinion is of the last episode of *Necroman*.'

I had never seen *Necroman*, as we don't have a TV, but he was so interested in his subject that I didn't have the heart to tell him.

'Brilliant,' I said. 'Brutal, mind you, and pornographic—but adultly so.' He looked pleased, and made lots of little marks on a chart in coloured inks.

'Ware lat zitcher see. Yair swee feel *Necroman* is reel adult entertainment. In fac my cummany spraird to be associated with *Necroman*. Nowper fessor, fewdone mine, arl leave this questionnaire with youffra feud eyes. Now hair batterfye call again say neck Smundy—no, Mundy's a puppy-collared eye. Say nex Chewsdy? Bat the same time? Or rat-shorken venience. Youjah say Wendell sou chew, anarl fit in. A corsile liaise with your seckertry. A now fewdone mine…' He started to open up further compartments in his case. How was I to get rid of him? He was indefatigable and apparently immovable. He was talking briskly about categories of viewers, and the social implications of *Necroman*. He explained also that his client's product washed out trapped grease by means of pulsier mini-bubbles, and that it was in every way a superior product, as was only to be expected from the sponsors of such adult entertainment as *Guess Whom*.

He continued to ask questions which I answered to the best of my ability, or rather in such a way as to cause a minimum of comment and delay. He filled in his charts and forms with lightning speed, and kept thanking me for being soak woprative.

'And now'—he turned to me with a bright, sentimental smile—'Hammany kiddies?'

I was about to supply him with the fictitious information he so obviously craved when Miss Nibbly appeared at the doorway. 'Skew smee, professor,' she said, scratching her ear with a pencil, 'but there's a gentleman atside, waiting to see you.' She looked a little uncomfortable. 'I think he's a policeman,' she added slowly.

'Good,' I said. 'Show him in right away. I'll be delighted to give him any information I can about this brutal murder. Mr Hoomit, I'm afraid I'll have to ask you to leave. This is a matter of life and death. The Assistant Commissioner needs my help. You'll appreciate that I cannot possibly keep him waiting. I'm sorry but you'll have to leave immediately. Yes, yes, I know; the questionnaire. Just give it to Miss Nibbly on your way out.' I picked up his adding machine and crammed it into his case. The various loose papers, graphs and charts which he had strewn all over my desk I forced into his hands, into his pockets—anywhere. In a matter of a few seconds I had him completely packed up, out of the door and on his way. I sank back in the chair and sighed with relief. Thank heavens, peace at last. Now, I suppose I'd better see this new visitor. I laughed to myself. I wondered who this 'policeman' would turn out to be. Life assurance, perhaps, or encyclopaedias.

A tall, heavily built man entered the room, followed by two more of equal omnipotence and menace. 'Professor Lauder,' he said, 'I want to ask you a few questions in connection with the discovery, in this building early this morning, of a dismembered female torso…'

Such a Good Boy

He never said 'Die' to the living.
He never said 'Scat' to a cat.
He never said 'Boo' to a kangaroo.
He never did this—or that.

He always kept clear of propellers;
Never spoke to the man at the wheel.
He always said 'Thanks' to people in banks,
And always took food with his meal.

He never took umbrage, or opium,
Or ran round the rugged rocks.
He never missed school, or acted the fool
And always wore woollen socks.

He never sat on a tuffet,
Or pulled out a plum with his thumb;
And never, in churches, left ladies in lurches;
Or opened the OP rum.

He never pinched little girls' bottoms,
Or peered down the front of their necks;
Considered it folly to covet a dolly,
Or think of the opposite sex.

He never did anything nasty.
He never got stinking, or cried;
Unmarred by one speckle, a permanent Jekyll,
With never a shadow of Hyde.

He never called anyone 'Drongo',
Or even ate peas with a knife.
He never crossed swords with the overlords;
Such a good boy all his life.

When he finally died and was buried
His loving ones tried to mourn;
They put at his head a tablet which read,
'Here he lies, but why was he born?'

The Strine Song

Tim Pannelli, the famous poet and songwriter, telephoned me recently and asked if he might call and see me; he wanted my advice about a Strine song he had written. Naturally, I told him I'd be delighted, and so here he was now in my office. I had, of course, read most of Pannelli's work, including the many historical dramas for which he is famous, but until now I had never had the pleasure of meeting this great man.

Tim Pannelli is a most unusual-looking man. Powerfully built, and I would think at least seven feet tall in his stockinged feet, he is not handsome in the usual sense of the word, but he is certainly impressive.

As I rose to greet him I noticed that his open, friendly face was marred by an ugly welt of scar tissue across the forehead, caused, I later discovered, by his continual failure to stoop when passing through doorways. Apart from that, his head appeared to be one of the standard, unshrunken ones, with the finely chiselled nose and all that. One could see immediately that here was a great artist, a dedicated poet. He was smoking an extraordinarily malodorous cigar, and he had, apparently, recently consumed a fairly large amount of garlic.

'My dear Mr Pannelli,' I said. 'This is a great pleasure.'

He smiled in response to my greeting, and I noticed the elegant crenellations of his mossy nicoteeth.

'No, no, Professor Lauder,' he replied, 'the pleasure is mine. It's very good of thou to see me. I know thou must be a very busy man.'

I was momentarily puzzled by his use of the second-person singular, and then I remembered all those historical dramas.

'I am most anxious,' he continued, 'to have thy expert criticism. This is my first song in Strine and, as thou know, it's not an easy language.'

'Of course,' I said. 'But do sit down. Will you have a cup of coffee or a three-course meal or something?' I was hoping to be able to detach him from that cigar, which was about ten inches long and as black as licorice.

'No thank thee—just had lunch.' He exhaled enthusiastically. I opened the windows. He continued: 'Well, I mustn't take up too much of thy time. To work, to work.' He patted his pockets, searching for his song. There was something magnetic about the man's personality; one couldn't help liking him, in spite of the cigar.

'Ah, here it is,' he cried. 'Oh, and have some of this. Very good for thee.' He offered me a handful of garlic.

'No thanks, just had lunch,' I said.

'Well, if thou are ready, I'll sing it now. Thou haven't a piano, have thou? No? Never mind.'

'Just a moment,' I said. 'Do you mind if I call my assistant? I know he would want to hear this. And Miss Nibbly, too. They'd never forgive me if I didn't share this unique experience with them.' I called Miss Nibbly and asked her to tell Dr Paragon to come in. I introduced everyone, and then we all sat down on the floor at Pannelli's stockinged feet.

He drew himself up to his full height, and held out his bit of paper at arm's length. He paused for a moment, then took a deep breath.

'One, two, three, testing,' he sang in a surprisingly light, clear tenor voice. 'One, two, three, testing. How's that, okay?'

'Magnificent,' I said. Dr Paragon nodded his head.

'Skew smee,' said Miss Nibbly, 'you've got a rarely laughly voice, Mr Pannelli, but I rarely think it'd sand even better if you took out your cigar. Don't you think so, Dr Paragon?'

Andy looked up from the hot dog he was eating. 'Yair, stairfnittly,' he said. 'Yair sam daddedly. Snow datter battered.'

Pannelli removed his cigar from his mouth and put it down carefully on the edge of the desk, where it continued to crackle briskly. 'Okay,' he said, 'let's go. "With Air Chew". That's the title of the song—"With Air Chew". Ah one, ah two, ah three, ah four.' And he started to sing.

With air chew, with air chew,
Iker nardly liver there chew,
An I dream a badger kisser snite and die.
Phoney wicked beer loan,
Jars-chewer mere nonnair roan,
An weed dreamer batter mooner pinner sky.

With air chew, with air chew,
Hair mike-owner liver there chew?
Wile yerrony immy dream sigh maulwye scrine.
Anna strewer seffner barf,
Yuma snow-eye Nietzsche laugh,
Cars with air chew immy arm sit snow-ewe Strine.

When he had finished there was a long silence. I think we were all too overcome by our feelings to applaud. Miss Nibbly had broken down completely, and was sobbing and blowing her nose. Even Dr Paragon, who ordinarily doesn't show any emotion other than impatience, was visibly affected. He sniffed hard, and surreptitiously brushed away a tear with the back of his hot dog. It was a moving and memorable experience. In the general commotion, while we were all scrambling to our feet, and coughing and carrying on, I removed the great man's cigar from my desk and dropped it into a filing cabinet.

We all crowded around him and patted him on the back and congratulated him. Miss Nibbly asked for his autograph, and Dr Paragon offered him a chlorophyll tablet.

'Ye think it's okay, then?' asked Pannelli.

'Truly magnificent,' I said. 'I wouldn't think of altering a word of it. And I must compliment you on your Strine accent. Remarkable.'

Miss Nibbly blew her nose again, and went to get some coffee.

'Thou don't think the title is perhaps a little too—ah, abrupt? I had thought of calling it "Phoney Eiche Daffer Latin Slamp".'

'No, I wouldn't touch it,' I said. '"With Air Chew" is just right; so much more direct; so poignant.' I kept on talking, to keep his mind from his cigar, but already he was patting his pockets again. Fortunately Miss Nibbly came in before he could light up, and we all sat down and drank the coffee, and talked about 'With Air Chew'.

'Welimer sconow,' said Dr Paragon, finally breaking it up. 'Car morn Philippa, back twirk. Well taddar sport. Be senior.'

The spell was broken. Pannelli looked at his watch.

'Well,' he said, 'thank thee again for all thy advice and encouragement. Thou've been most helpful.' He shook me warmly by both hands, and left. There was a dull thud of bone on architrave as he reached the doorway outside.

WITH AIR CHEW

Vivace (♩=138)

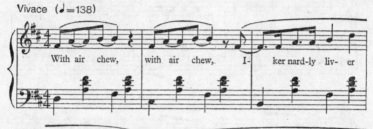

With air chew, with air chew, I- ker nard-ly liv- er

the-r- e chew, An I dream a bad-ger kiss-er snite and die.

Pho- ney wic-ked be- er loan

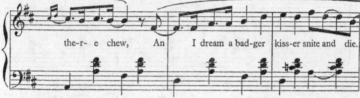

.... Jars chew-er me-re non-nair roan .... An

weed dream-er bat-ter moon-er pin- ner sky.

With air chew, with air chew, Hair mike-ow-ner liv-er

the-r-e chew? Wile yer-ro-ny im-my dream sigh maul-wye scrine

.... An-na strew-er seff-ner barf .... Yu-

ma snow-eye Nie-tzsche laugh, Cars with air chew im-.my

arm sit snow-ewe Strine.

Nose Tone Unturned

And the Secretary is desirous (the letter went on to say, as well as I remember) that I should inform you of the Minister's appreciation of the valuable contribution you are making to a wider understanding of our glorious heritage—the Strine language. He refers, in particular, to a public statement you have recently made to the effect that all literature addressed to intending migrants to Australia should be published in two languages, English and Strine. And so on. It was signed by Victor Cluster, First Assistant Secretary of the Department of Inducement and Assimilation.

I had pointed out, in my statement to the press, that the initial dismay and subsequent disillusion of some newly arrived migrants to this country could be obviated by making it clear to them, before they leave their native land, that although English is the official, written language of this country, the unofficial, spoken language is Strine.

Anyway, the Minister had, it seems, decided to take the matter up and, to use his own unique and tersely cogent phrase, to 'leave no stone unturned'. I was invited to Canberra to discuss the matter and, after due deliberation, to make detailed recommendations to the Minister.

I managed to have a few words with Dr Cluster before the others arrived. He told me that the only other persons who would be attending this initial discussion would be the chairman, Professor Mingle, representing the Minister; Professor Blare of Airdelight University; and, of course, himself. He warned me quietly that Professor Blare was not a particularly easy man to get along with. 'In fact he's an intractable bloody nong,' he said tactfully. 'But the Minister feels that he might well be able to make a valuable contribution because of his particularly pure Strine accent.'

He had barely finished speaking, and the word 'nong' was still echoing among the teacups, when the door was flung open, and Professor Blare, followed by an already rather desperate-looking chairman, burst into the room. He threw his hat onto the desk, knocking over a large silver-framed portrait of Mrs Cluster with a spaniel. He shook Dr Cluster's hand so boisterously that I could hear the bones crunching like biscuits. He ignored me completely. He stumbled over a chair, tore at his collar, and shouted, 'Now Warsaw liss Strine chairs? I carmike hatter tiler fit. A noo sis Zafflepock repbairg, or worreffris snime is? Dar sneeno hatter spairl?' We were off to a very inauspicious start.

There was a lot of embarrassed shuffling and coughing, and Dr Cluster tried to disappear into the floor. I could see now what he had meant; but Professor Blare, for all his madcap gaucherie, might well turn out to be very valuable indeed; his accent was bang-on.

While I was saying hello to Professor Mingle, I saw Dr Cluster saying a few quiet words into Professor Blare's whiskery ear. He immediately turned to me with an enormous glary, foxy grin, and crushed my hand in his instant meatpress.

'Sorry, mate,' he screamed with laughter, sucking in great bagfuls of air through his clacky tombstone teeth, and showering out spluttery droplets all over my face. 'Dint Noah's you mate. Glatter meecher. An woss your rill nime? Carmorn carmorn dopey shy.' He jabbed at my sternum with a case-hardened forefinger, and leered at me with pale-blue popping eyes.

'Well, actually…' I started to tell him, but he was off again, fizzing about the room, waving his arms, knocking things over, and telling some long, unfunny story about his wartime sex life. 'An theshy wars praggly nygerd…' he was saying. Eventually he was brought under control by the chairman, and we got down to work.

After the preliminary formalities, I was asked if I would elaborate on the statement I had already made. We each had a copy of this in front of us, but of course Blare hadn't read his, and we had to wait while he wrestled with it noisily; squirming, clearing his throat and scratching at his crusty, sunburnt scalp. He looked up every now and then, as if he found our silence unbearable, and bared his tigerish fangs, and said, 'Haaaaa, Haaaaaaam, Ha!' Then he would suck in some more air, and get down again to his task. I don't think he got past the first paragraph—in fact I wonder, now, if he can read. But he put on a good show. After a few minutes he placed the paper slowly and deliberately on the table in front of him; he lifted his hands high into the air, very quickly, as though he had just completed building a house of cards. He slapped his thighs triumphantly, and said, 'Haaaaaaa!' and with the back of his hand he wiped his chin with the wild flourish of someone escaping from slavery, and again he said, 'Haaaaaaa!' He must have used up more energy in five minutes than anyone else would in a week. The chairman caught my eye.

'Well, gentlemen,' I said, 'I have nothing to add to the statement in front of you. I believe, however, that with Professor Blare's help I can make out a fairly strong case for bilingual literature for migrants. I propose to take at random a few typical situations, such as a newcomer might be expected to encounter, and—well, just let's see what happens.'

Professor Blare, I noticed, had temporarily abandoned the realistic drawing he had been working on of a naked woman, and was now chewing busily at a loose thread at his shirt-cuff button. He bit it off and spat it out noisily. He looked up as I paused; he obviously hadn't listened to a word I had been saying.

'Wossat, mate?' He held up his drawing for everyone to admire, and screamed with laughter. 'Noppaird, eh?'

'Well,' I continued, 'first of all, let us imagine, say, a young English girl (Blare looked up quickly, eyebrows raised), new to this country and recently married to an Australian. It is the middle of the night. Suddenly she sits up in bed in their new home somewhere in the outer suburbs. She is nervous; she thinks she has heard someone at the door. Okay? Got that, professor?'

'Look, snore ma juice cowny gone me, mate. You know youger tadder the wire these sorter things.' He scratched his leg cruelly, and went back to his drawing—flowerpots now, and little squares with dots in them.

The chairman looked tired. Cluster was drumming his fingertips softly on the table.

'Well,' I battled on, wondering if we'd be given a drink before lunch, 'well, if she were still at home at Surbiton or Welwyn Garden City, what would she say to her husband in this situation? She'd say: George, there's someone there. Now who can that be, knocking on the door at this time of night? It's half past two! But if she says this to her Australian husband he just looks at her blankly and goes back to sleep. Naturally, the poor girl is then overwhelmed by despondency and alarm, and starts to make plans to go home to Mum and the smog. What has happened is that her husband doesn't know what she's saying because she has been talking English instead of Strine.'

I paused, to let this sink in. Professor Blare's stomach rumbled violently. 'Pahn *mee*!' he said.

'Now, professor, if I may have your attention for a moment, what should she have said?'

He looked at me as though I had just arrived from Mars. 'Wossat, mate?'

Then, suddenly, I thought I could see how it might be done. 'Professor,' I said, 'would you please just repeat what I say?'

'Okay, sport. Any time.'

'George,' I said, 'there's someone at the door outside.'

'Where, mate?' He looked over his shoulder.

'No, no, professor. Just repeat what I say. Right? George, there's someone at the door outside.'

'George.' He stopped. No one moved. Somewhere, in the passage outside, a pin dropped. He looked at us each in turn. Slowly, he smiled.

'George,' he said, 'the summer gnat the door rat's-eyed.'

'Oh, wonderful!' I said. 'Good!' Everyone relaxed. The chairman lit a cigarette.

'Now, are you ready? Now who can that be, knocking on the door at this time of night?'

'Nahoogen thappy,' said the professor, 'nogger nonner dort this timer night? Haaaaa. Hmmmmm. Haaaaaaam!' At last he appeared to have caught on; he had even stopped squirming.

'It's half past two,' I said.

'Note za-pa sleffen mate,' he said, looking at his watch.

'No, no, professor. Just repeat what I say. Go and see who it is, George, it must be important.'

'Norm,' said the professor, 'it zapa stoo. Goan see hootiz, Norm. Muspeem pawnt.' He paused, and added anxiously, 'Mipey re lurgent!'

He was inspired. How could he possibly have known that the Strine for George is Norm? Pure intuition, obviously. I took a quick look at the others. Dr Cluster's joyful mouth was wide open. Professor Mingle was leaning back with his eyes closed, his hands folded across his stomach. He looked as though he were listening to Mozart.

'Ready, professor? Now—We've got a new car, Betty. You wouldn't believe it would you?'

'Weegar newgar, Cherryl. You woomba leaver twoocha? Carmen air flooker tit.' He was really in the groove now. 'A mitre mine scotter new Vailiant.' His eyes had taken on a fixed and glassy look.

'What did he do with the old car?' I asked.

'Thair tole hape? Eager tridderfit.' His eyes were rolling back into his head and he appeared to be going into some sort of trance. I thought I would try him on some more advanced stuff. 'Where,' I said, 'is the pen of my aunt?'

'Wezzme Auntie Spiro?'

'There's no drink left, Doris.'

'We fra natter grog, Sandra.' He was now in a deep trance. I whispered to the chairman, and Dr Cluster tiptoed out and came back with a tape recorder. Now we were really in business.

'There's no more pudding, dear,' I said, in a high, feminine falsetto.

'Welker knife some bren jairm then, marm?' He jiggled an invisible yo-yo with a rigid right arm. 'An marm marm. War wego navver tea, marm?' And so it went on.

By about six o'clock we had all had enough. The three of us were sprawled at the table, finishing off the last of a bottle of scotch. The professor was lying on the floor in a coma.

Jack (Professor Mingle) sat up and yawned slowly. He stretched himself and rolled down his sleeves. Vic Cluster held the bottle up to the light, then he put on his shoes.

'Well, gentlemen,' said the chairman, putting on his coat, and tugging at his tie. 'A very fruitful day. The Minister will be delighted.' He looked anxiously at Professor Blare, who had now begun to snore gently and was, I was relieved to see, scratching himself in his sleep. His lips were twitching, like a dreaming dog's.

We all looked at each other. Vic hid the glasses and the empty bottle, and tidied up the room. Then he went over and shook the professor gently.

'Wake up, professor,' he said quietly. 'Time to catch your plane soon.'

The professor stirred, and opened his pale blue eyes. He sat up slowly. 'Woskoa non?' he asked.

'You had a bit of a blackout, professor,' I told him. 'Nothing serious, but we thought you ought to rest for a while. How do you feel now?'

'Noppaird, mate. Not reel bad.' He looked at us all suspiciously, then at his watch. 'Neely ah-pa *seeegs*!' he screeched. 'I carber leevit.' He got slowly to his feet. He looked a bit staggery. I would never have believed he could be so subdued.

We got him a cup of coffee, and he finished off the remains of some sandwiches. Gradually he came back to life. We all went off to the airport together and, by the time his plane had arrived, he was right back in top form; talking our heads off, booming and spluttering, and sucking at his great sharky fangs.

Strine Rhymes for Kiddies

Rider cock horse to Nyngan or Nome,
To seer fine lady clee natter Rome;
Mo Nyngan grow Nyngan fee tawler blister,
Sheesha lav music upon a transistor.

Little Chair Corner come blow your horn,
An dofer get those sharps and flats,
Ando calm beckon Christma Smorn
In wunner those silly paper hats.

The war slittle chap, panny adder little nap,
An his dinner was long overdone.
His good wife Nelly was stillet the telly,
With Astroboy, Steptoe and Son.

Hi diddle diddle, Little Jenny Baker.
Heigh ho! says Rowley, waddle-eye do with me pence?
Me mumma wozza Quaker; tiger ruppen shaker;
Now say it all again slowly;
It doesn't seem to scan or even make sense.

Ordeal by Earbash

'Well yugen dooitcher like,' said Dr Paragon, in his usual uncompromising manner. 'Zarf trawlitz your show. Bargee, mite, I moany triner mica teasier.'

'Yes, I know, Andy,' I said, 'and I appreciate your thoughtfulness on my behalf, but…'

'Listen, mite,' he cut in, 'I jar swan a get it over. Iger tarder Stan a *nar* Paula time. Orlis farsova a lotta mygrinse. Y. carnay learner talk Strine before they *car* mere?'

'Okay,' I said. 'Put it down with the others.'

He lowered the large notice he had been holding up over his head, and banged it down onto the floor. He stood there, muttering, and waving the blood back into his hands. 'Thing kyle goa navver bye tweet,' he said. *'Ear* fats okay with *ewer* course,' he added with heavy sarcasm.

'Yes, Andy, you go and have some lunch.'

'Seer lighter then.' He went off, muttering something about aorta do this and Y. carnay do that.

I turned the notice around and propped it up against the wall so that it faced into the room. I stood well back and looked at it critically. Yes, it looked about right to me. It was one of a series of bilingual notices which I was preparing, at the request of the Department of Inducement and Assimilation, for display in Australia House, in London. Now that the authorities had decided, at last, that all official signs and notices in this country were to be in two languages, English and Strine, it was important that intending migrants to Australia should be given, in advance, some idea of the sort of thing they could expect to be confronted by on arrival.

The notice in front of me was three feet wide by two feet deep, with black lettering on a brilliant yellow ground.

The English wording appeared immediately above the Strine translation:

NO ADMITTANCE
Key Powder Vere—Penalty £5
$10

The $10 had purposely been lettered in a different style from the remainder of the wording, and had been placed out of alignment, so as to give the whole thing an official, asymmetric, authoritative appearance.

I looked at my watch. I'd have to skip lunch; Kangruskin would be here soon. I asked Miss Nibbly to get me a baked bean and potato salad sandwich, on white bread, and a carton of lemon-flavoured milk—the usual professorial snack. Then I stood all the notices up, side by side against the walls, and sat back and admired them while I waited for my sandwich.

Eli Kangruskin's background was something of a mystery. He had told me that his father was a Russian, and his mother Hungarian; that he had been born in Paris, and had spent most of his childhood travelling with his parents all over Europe, and in this way had learned to speak ten languages. I had heard elsewhere that he was born in Liverpool, and that his parents were Greek. Whatever the facts were, he certainly spoke at least ten European languages—each with the accent of the country he had just previously left. He spoke Italian like a native—a native, that is, of Copenhagen. He spoke practically no Strine at all, presumably because he was still here in Australia. He had arrived in this country a few years ago, having come from Birmingham or somewhere, where he had been engaged, so he said, in some top-secret liaison work for the British government. In Australia he had worked at a number of different jobs: growing mushrooms in a disused tunnel, driving a bulldozer, sandpapering the lips of window display models, stringing beads, and running what he called a 'fish coffee'. Finally he had joined the Department as a specialist in languages; and now, today, he was here to go through this latest batch of notices. I had found him, during our brief association, to be co-operative and friendly, and we got on quite well together. However, he seemed to get on Dr Paragon's nerves—but then, who didn't? His main trouble was that once he started talking he was unable to stop, and what he had to say was not always relevant.

'He are, sport,' Andy was saying. 'Smoke? He are, air fwunner mine.'

'North airnx,' said Kangruskin. 'Ah dawn's mork. Munjew, woonts ah woss a gent's morka. Boot ah harder giffit oop; ah woss korphenorla tarm. Ahra mamba, one Sorbonne a tarm, whan ah woss a student in Paris, ah shed a flutt with a chupp called Funton. Chorlie Funton. Eeeeee, he wosser narse chupp. Well, woun dair—it wosser Moondair; ahra mamba it wosser Moondair because it was rairnen...' He was off to his usual flying start.

'Here's the next one, Frad,' I said. He had asked me to call him Frad, although his name was supposed to be Eli. He said all his France called him Frad. I drew his attention, such as it was, to the notice:

BEWARE OF ONCOMING TRAFFIC
War Chaffer Ong-calming Veagles

'Ooooo! Fair skluss,' said Kangruskin. 'Fair skluss. Remarned smee offer tarm wenwee webber harnd the larns utter plairce colled Doonkairk— you mayor foorder fit. Anywhere, we werrin dairnger of bing cuptured. Muppler toon hud joospin...'

'Yes, yes, okay sport,' broke in Andy, impatient as ever but trying, not very successfully, to conceal it. 'Fit sorla sime to you—hair bat jar sketter non wither business in hairnd?' He held the next notice up in front of Kangruskin's nose:

PLEASE DO NOT SMOKE
Nouse mogen!

'Norse Morgan,' said Kangruskin. 'Eeeeee! Fair skluss. Air worn! Core Sardon's mork mussall. Booter ramamba, a frantomarn…It woss whan ah wossin Frimmundle. This chupp wosser grairt frand—an awl frantomarn. Anywhere, he yoost to smawg a parp. Well wound air, he was teginny swarf…Munjew, he harden bin murried morna coopler moonce. His warf snairm, fie ramamba corrairctly, woss Gluddis. Well, anywhere…'

'Next one, Andy, please,' I said. One thing about Kangruskin—he didn't mind in the least being interrupted, or even ignored. Just as long as he had a face near him—even a good photograph would do—he'd go on talking.

PLEASE DO NOT SPIT
Do Not Spit!

'Saw anywhere…arsy stairpt insard, soodenleh orla lart scare-morn. Unna corsy got soocha frarty brawkie sparp. Snupp kleenorfinny stairth. Kloock! Anywhere, the neg stair—it wosser Soondair. Und soy sair twis warf, he sairt, Gluddis, he sairt, he sairt, Gluddis, arf brawken me parp, a nitzer Soondair…'

'Or geemite, car morn, car morn, zarp tew. Gaudy drivey arp the wall.' Andy appeared to be losing control. 'Hi, you! Jar sloogered the notice willier? Look! Jar slemmy poodger inner pidger. Gawd, I mire swell noppy hear. Torga bat disinterested…'

VISITORS ARE REQUESTED
NOT TO WALK ON THE LAWNS
Key Porpha Gra Smite—
An Don't Pigger Flares

Kangruskin nodded in a vague way at the wording. I don't think he was aware now of anything but the magic of his own monologue. Andy had to, or thought he had to, prod him in the chest. 'See? Key porpha gra smite!' he shouted in his face. 'Lougar fattabatta narf a this; woddsy thinky *zear* for?'

'Ooooo! Eeeeee! Fair skluss! Anywhere, Gluddis—yus, thutt wosser nairm, Gluddis. Ahra mamba naw, Gluddis. Anywhere, arsett wosser Soondair, orla poobs wek lawsed. Well, anywhere—ooooo, it mooster bin a coopler moon slairter, wenner woss buck in Frimmundle. Nought mooster bin foor moon slairter; ahra mamba because it wosser Wairn-stair un ah woss barn a noo oomprulla. Eeeee, nought lark the awld worn thaw. Or naw, nought lark the awld worn. The awld worn wosser leetle fawlder narp worn. It tairter leetle norp on the hundle. Here, I shaw you. Dew huffer bit a pairper? Uh leetle silfer norp...'

DANGER! SUPRNTNDNT TRNSPT RESRCH STN
Loogairdy Dome Bycher!

This one had been Andy's contribution, and consequently he had a proprietary attitude towards it. 'Look, sport,' he said slowly, enunciating each syllable with great care, 'Jar stoomie a fiver willier? Jar sloogered the bloody notice, and let sav your ont's depinion. Neff my norlis Gludd-dis bull.'

He had loosened his collar and tie, and was breathing hard and muttering, 'Gordger woomba leaver twoocha? Anew tell me I undress to mate his intelligence. Hi! You! *Look!*' He shouted, and jumped up and down.

Then he put his fingers into his mouth and let out an ear-splitting whistle. I sometimes wonder about Andy; probably something to do with his toilet training. Or perhaps it's his glands. Anyway, whatever the initial cause may have been, his top, today, was rapidly approaching blowpoint.

DANGER!
KEEP CLEAR OF THE PROPELLORS
Hey, Ewes!
Yorpha Bittner Go Nither Skruse

'But wed a Mormon tum's tairl you. Heewee were bug in Fairness. You naw, Fairness? All Fairness—E. Neatly? Anywhere, arse aired to this chupp—this corned lair chupp. Arse air twim, uss-et, we warner gorta the Dodger's Pulse, ussairt. But or liquored sair woss, Cissy Norrie, Cissy Norrie. Itcher's captain sairn cissy norrie cissy norrie cissy norrie. Urn paw awl Chorlie Funton—corsy woss blarn droonk, munjew—blarn droonk. He kep sairny waunted fallen tears. Ah worn fallen tears, he sairt. Men, he sairt. He sairt, Men, ah Moor-stuffer bort fife fallen tears. Naw ah usk you! Saw you naw wodder sair twim? Heh, heh, heh. Ah sair twim. Heh heh heh… Naw you womb Belair fit. Buttered straw…a new mare quart me. Arset, cissy norrie cissy norrie cissy norrie. Heeeeeeeeee, heeeeeeeeee, heeeeeeeeee… Dog abort luff…'

IT IS REGRETTED THAT, OWING TO CIRCUMSTANCES BEYOND THE JURISDICTION OF THIS DEPARTMENT, FURTHER INFORMATION HAS BECOME TEMPORARILY NON-AVAILABLE TO APPLICANTS
Gnome or Gnus!
Calm Bear Klyter!

FRAFFLY WELL SPOKEN

FRAFFLY WELL SPOKEN

How to Speak the Language
of London's West End

Afferbeck Lauder

*Professor of Strine Studies,
University of Sinny;*

*Fellow of the Yarnurdov Foundation,
London*

Illustrated by *Al Terego*

Acknowledgments

The author expresses his grateful thanks to the people of London, whose existence made this book possible.

He also expresses his warmest thanks to Mr Alistair Morrison for his invaluable criticism and advice throughout its compilation.

Foreword

Many of those discoveries which have led to an increased understanding of man and his environment have been the result of quite fortuitous and unpredictable occurrences. The bath-born Archimedean screw; gravity and the apple falling from Newton's tree; the boiling kettle which led to the steam engine and to Stephenson's 'Rocket'—these are well-known examples of minor events which have changed the course of history. More recently, a similar, and perhaps even more dramatic, enlargement of man's intellectual horizon has been the birth of Strine, which came about when Miss Monica Dickens, the British author, was autographing books in a shop in Sydney, Australia, and mistook the immortal words 'Emma Chissit' for a woman's name; not realising that this is Strine for 'How much is it?'

Professor Afferbeck Lauder read a report of this incident, and, in one of those flashes of revelation which are the hallmark of genius, saw at once that Australians are not, as everyone had until then thought, an English-speaking people after all; but that they only think they speak English.

Now Professor Lauder has discovered that a similar situation exists in the West End of London. Here, he tells us (and this, his latest work, proves it beyond doubt) we speak not English, but *Fraffly*.

Who knows what radical changes in British customs and attitudes this discovery will bring in its train? Where will it all end? Only the master himself can tell us—and his answer is: York air scissors good as mine.

Alistair Morrison
London, 1968

Introduction

Fraffly, the language spoken in the West End of London, takes its name from the expression 'Fraffly caned a few,' meaning 'Frightfully (i.e. very) kind of you,' and from the many variants of this expression, such as 'Fraffly caned a fume shore' and 'Fraffly nacer few.'

A characteristic feature of Fraffly is that it is thought, not only by those who speak it, but also by those to whom it is spoken, to be English. This is not an unusual phenomenon; Australians, who speak Strine, also think they are speaking English; and a similar misapprehension exists in America. Normally this creates neither confusion nor dismay; it is only when two of these cultures impinge upon one another that the trouble starts. Just how great the resulting confusion may then be can easily be discovered by anyone who will listen, for example, to an American tourist trying to buy hominy grits in Piccadilly, or to an immigrant from London, newly arrived in Sydney, searching for winkles or a regimental tie.

But these experiences, heartbreaking though they may be to those involved, are of minor importance when seen against the background of international politics, when the subject under discussion may be the closing of a canal, the position of a national boundary, or the sale of arms. Here, the fact that both the negotiators think that they are speaking English, but are not, could lead to who knows what disastrous 'incident'. It is in an attempt to obviate such dangerous situations, and to bring about closer international understanding, that this book has been compiled.

Afferbeck Lauder
Boggly Square, London, 1968

Fraffly Well Spoken

–air; –eh: Interchangeable suffixes (corresponding to the English *–y*) as in: Complittlair; extroddnerreh; etc. Occasionally the archaic *–y* is still used, although pronounced *–air* or *–eh*, as in the word *Fraffly*. As there does not appear to be any reason for the retention of the archaic form, it is assumed that it is an example of British conservatism, like the veal and ham pie, for the continued production of which there can also surely be no valid reason.

Ashel; Ashered: I shall; I should. As in: 'Ashel beer term letter the sivvning'; 'This food's a disgress; ashel bring it op in the House'; 'Ashered lake to nir whey'; or 'Ashered of thotty would hef bin myrrh skretful.'

Assay: I say. As in: 'Assay earl chep, euchre noddleh dwenthing else'; or 'Assay earl kell, water chollicker dead ear.'

Beddleh: Disastrously; shockingly; desperately. As in: 'What the skontreh beddleh nids is another Chodgell,' or 'Chol skemmof rother beddleh. Fell don fay fletser stezz 'n' brirker coppler legs. Nothing motcha coss, but he was beddleh shecken.'

Belliff: A particular kind of furniture remover; also a leaf of laurel, used in cooking *awkstel* and other dishes.

Bessa Clare: Fundamentally, basically. As in: 'The tropple, bessa clare, is that he has nir censer fumah. Quetterness chepper koss, but withar chooma.'

Blemmer; Blemmim: Blame her or him. As in: 'Wong con blemmer, relleh, when one nerzer bare crond.'

Brishempah, the: That particular group of peoples and territories once under the sovereign dominion of Britain. It no longer exists, but its passing is still occasionally lamented.

Chezz; Chozzle: (*Sometimes also:* Chairs). Your good health! Cheers! As in: 'Nozz the tem frolgered men to compter the edda the potty. Chozzle man! Chozz!'

Cod: A large inedible fish; also a small piece of stiffened paper on which may be printed a message, or symbols, e.g. Christmas cods; purse cods; pleng cods, on which appear speds, hots, dammonds and clopse; itsquay tonna cods; and 'Ditchy liver cod?'

Common Simian: Fraffly contains many English words, of which *common* and *simian* are but two. This phrase does not, however, mean either 'vulgar' or 'apelike'; it is a form of apology, addressed to someone who has asked for help, but for whom no immediate help is intended, other than an introduction to a third person, who will then introduce him to a fourth person, who will then introduce him to a fifth—and so on until the nth person supplies the, by then much needed, help. 'Common simian a wicker so; omshore wilpy ebble to fix something. Kip in todge' means, very often, no more than just 'Common simian a wicker so.' The usual sequence is somewhat as follows.

Andrew felt in his pocket for another sixpence. He turned to the back of his diary and found the next number. Here it was—Edward Fingerpost, Fraffly 1212. He lifted the receiver and waited for the dialling tone. Edward had said to him, 'Common simian a wicker so, earl man. See war twicken do.' Okay, Andrew said to himself, we'll see war chooken do. He found, already, after only a few short weeks back in London, that he was starting to think in Fraffly again. Just as well, really; this business of finding a job was turning out to be more difficult than he had expected. There always seemed to be some sort of barrier between him and that interesting, well-paid job which he knew he'd be able to hold down so easily—once it was his. But the trouble in London was that you could never pin anyone down; never say what you had to say—just this never-ending series of luncheons. Anyway, he'd keep trying. He took a deep breath of what was left of the air in the telephone box, dialled the number, and waited.

'Fingerpost & Fellermangle. G'monning. May herlpew?'

'May I speak to Mr Fingerpost, please? This is Andrew Finch.' He hoped that wasn't too blunt; perhaps he should have said 'actually' somewhere in the middle of it.

'Freddy snore tinter dare.'

'Oh! He was expecting a call from me. He said to ring about ten.'

'Stmerment pliz.' (Pause.) 'You themster Finch? Am trannock neck jaw.' A click, and he was through.

'Undraw! Naster hiffem yaw.' Edward's voice came through loud and clah. What was this business of not being in today? Andrew again wondered why the switch girls, always and everywhere in London, were given instructions to say that Mr So-and-so was not in, was out of town, was not back from lunch, was away until Tuesday, or in a conference and couldn't be disturbed. How differently, he thought, they do things here.

'Hello, Ted—I mean Edward. How are you? I was wondering if by any chance you'd…um, ah…' He paused. He couldn't very well say, 'Well, can you give me a job?' He had quickly learned that such a question would be very much worse than useless. Like asking someone if their sex life was satisfactory or, even worse, how much money they made. No, in London only the indirect approach brought results—and the more indirect the better.

'…thought we might have a bit of lunch,' he found himself saying once more.

'Ah, stmermen turl chepp. Staffer look 'n' see. Hmm…Yes, good. Wheshel we meet?'

'I'll call at your office. About one?' At least, if he got there a bit early, there might be an opportunity to bring up the subject of a job.

He arrived at twenty to one, and was shown into Edward's office. Hello, Edward, nice to see you. Hello, Undraw, naster see yaw. A short exchange about the probability or otherwise of rain; then he said, 'I've been wondering, Edward, whether you've had any opportunity to give any thought to the possibility that perhaps you might see whether or not it might possibly be; of course I realise how extraordinarily busy you must be with all this expansion; but at the same time; I mean look at it this way; I mean an organisation such as yours must be continually on the lookout for well, ah; you no doubt remember that little matter we were discussing last time we had lunch together; after all with all the experience one has fortunately been able to be in a position to have the opportunity of acquiring over the past few years; I mean, one would imagine that a company such as this one, a progressive company with a policy of vigorous; I mean all these new branches you were telling me about; surely it must be very difficult, and particularly when one thinks of the pressure you must be under from the shareholders; hard to find the right men; I mean of the right calibre; after all, some of these young chaps; I know only too well from my own experience; straight from their; no experience at all, really, yet at the same time they think they know; must be a very difficult decision for you to have to make, and one which I should think you must find; if you know what I mean. I often wonder how you appear to manage it all so effortlessly.'

That should do it, he thought. Not bad, really. He felt, for the first time, that he was beginning to get the hang of it. Perhaps he had been just a shade too abrupt. Still, he could see that he was improving; he'd managed to say *almost* nothing relevant. Just to be on the safe side, he added, 'How's the golf?'

Edward's mask lit up. 'Jaw skotsom new clops. Joy good. Um… thought one might heffer word with Fettlehurst. Bleefie slooking for someone to tare curver Isbister's job. Stmerment. Fettlehurst, Broadglade, Hobbs and Wickle, you know.' He asked for the number.

*Well
lecture lair
Deddie's
a brokah,
but ed lake
to do
mottling*

Goo chur!
May earl
menza
plestic surchin
in Holly Street.
Youm
smittim

'Chollz!' Then, after an eighteen-hole postmortem, 'Chollz, one has heah, in one's office, a fay distinguished Orstrellion. Ware, lecture lair, he snore trelleh; he jar scot beckier. Thorcher mare; I mean this Isbister chepp. Well you know, old chepp. Good, ol posser tonn.' Then a recapitulation of the postmortem, and he hung up.

Edward was silent as they descended in the lift, and seemed pre-occupied. After they had walked a hundred yards or so, he turned to Andrew, and after some hesitation, said, 'Assay earl man, herpew dernt maned may seng this chew.' He hesitated, apparently embarrassed, and at a loss for the right words. 'Mospey freng call man. Herpew dernt maned. B'toff trol, ummint sair—yoomce nir war temmene. Dew maned if I *do* put it rother *bluntleh*? Um, ah…when you hair floncheon with Fettlehurst…What? Earce, of koss; Chewsdair, of koss. Any weh, teg made vace, earl chepp; dew mender fame brootleh frenk with yaw? Dernt ectualleh *say* anything abot a *job*, earl man. I mean, it wouldn't *do*! One has mentioned your nem twim, off trol. Shouldn't overdo if, fay were you.'

Connor Bess Street: Adjective, derived from the name of the famous Carnaby Street, W1, from whence emanate the outrageously colourful and excitingly ridiculous clothes worn by so many of the young people of London. As in: 'Of co shies fay Connor Bess Street, b'trelleh quetta nay skell.'

cottnent, The: The continent of Europe, but excluding the United Kingdom. The word 'cottnent' is usually spoken as though spelt with a lower-case initial; thus implying amused tolerance, such as one might feel towards a small, eccentric and (thank heaven) distant cousin. Geo-graphically, the UK is a part of Europe; but this is disputed by many.

Ever since the composition, in the eleventh century, of the first comic strip (i.e. the Bayeux Tapestry), the sport of laughing at, and being laughed at by, foreigners has continued without interruption. In those far-off times it was the British who were the foreigners—to the Normans, anyway. Now, of course, it is everybody else. The British, incidentally, are probably the last people left in the world with enough humour and detachment to be able to laugh at themselves. Or may this perhaps be because there are so many foreigners in Britain?

So much has already been said about the British attitude towards foreigners that any further comment about the subject here would be redundant. The only thing which remains to be pointed out is that there has recently been a perceptible change in this attitude towards those funniest of all foreigners—the inhabitants of the cottnent. This must surely be because of Britain's impending, or thought by some to be impending, entry into the Common Market. It would seem that, if Britain is, after all, to become a part of the cottnent, then it's time the cottnent was promoted. The word 'cottnent' is, then, of considerable historical interest, as it must surely disappear from the Fraffly vocabulary, and be replaced by the more appropriate and more dignified name *Yoorrp!* However, it is a slow process, and it will be a long time before the significance is lost of that well-known saying: When in Rome, do as the British do.

Dour Pitterby: Do appear to be. As in: 'Theh dour pitterby rother horsetail. Prep swiggered gwot the bare quare!' or 'You dour pitterby rother grubbeh. Prep shoosht warshaw hunts.'

Earce: Yes. As in: 'Earce, earce, thairk yaw'; 'Earce and nir' ; 'Earce, of koss'; etc.

Earls Cool: Description of the tie worn around the neck of one who wishes to be recognised as an ex-pupil of a particular educational establishment. 'Educational' is used here in its widest sense, as the subjects taught are not only academic but include: cricket (and its opposite, 'snort cricket'); stiffupperlippery (*q.v.*); university and club entrance techniques; and government. Understatement is also taught, but is forgotten by the time the earls cool tie wearer writes his inevitable memoirs.

Ears: Is. As in: 'One dozen trelleh care hooey ears'; or 'Hootsy thinky ears?'

Egg-wetter Gree: An expression of concurrence and agreement. As in: 'Em nogwet shorrif egg-wetter gree withol you sair, but ashel defend to your death may rate to say so.' Egg-wetter gree, like many other Fraffly expressions, may occasionally have a second, slightly different meaning. For example:

> Egg-wetter gree withol you sair.
> It splenfer wan a nolta see.
> The poin-shoe mecca clirras dair.
> Egg-wetter gree; egg-wetter gree.

> Wong kondra fewchaw ockument.
> Omshore we yolla gree, and know it.
> However, sir, this document
> (A fewla lommy) doesn't show it.

> Your logic and hypothesis,
> We yolla gree, kannoppy shecken.
> The minor point that bothers is
> Jaw smilly thatchew wommis tecken.

Fay: Very. As in: 'Shiss fay caned, and fay swit; aim fay fawn torfa.' (*See also* Fraffly, *with which this adverb is interchangeable.*)

Fay Nods: Art which is created for its own sake, rather than for useful application. Specifically: penting, scolpchah, droing, poitreh, mioosk, oggteckchah and the dremmetticods. The last listed of these, the dremmetticods, deserve more than casual mention, as it is here, on the *stetch*

Sholleh
Mother,
the sitch
weshen's
frott with
denture

Now Choll
steer,
Ay fernley
head
fay
feck lezz

(whether it be *drommer* or merely *thettah*) that Fraffly is heard in its purest, richest, and most mellifluous form. Take, for example, the following extract from nearly every West End production.

> Valerie: Oh, Chems! Herken yaw sessitcher thing? Un to mere fol pipple! Oh, Chems! Her coochoo?
> James: Sorriol kell. Worce rother bisstleh awf mare. Wonkets rother kerry dware et Thames. Fork if mare, Fellrair.

And again, this passage by that best-beloved playwright of all:

> If mioosk bither fuder floff, pleh yawn;
> Giff mih excesser fit, thutt, soffting,
> The yepper tet mare sicken, und sir day.
> Thott strenneken! Ear tedder deng fol;
> Er! it care maw mare ear leg a swit sond
> Thet brithes a pawn a benker fay, Oh let's,
> Stilling end giffing urda.

Femme et cesse eau: This odd phrase, obviously French in origin, and perhaps introduced by the Norman conquerors, no longer bears any semantic relationship to the French from which it is derived. Femme et cesse eau (pronounced *Fam eh sesso*) does not, as one might have thought, mean 'woman and stopping water'; it means: 'It is impossible for you to stop me from saying what I am about to say,' or 'I have now made my final pronouncement on the subject, and it would be futile for you to attempt to convince me that what I have said is inaccurate.' It may be heard in contexts such as: 'Femme et cesse eau, youf trop-chaw possel on meh foot. Herpew dernt maned,' meaning: 'Careful, there, you clumsy clot!' Or, again: 'Your weff slooking fay chommingt net, femme et cesse eau,' meaning: 'I see that your so-called wife is still the hideous old creep that she has been for so long; but I do not say this to you, as I need the increase in salary which I hope will be my reward for having to suffer the tedium of your presence and hers at this shambles on which you have bestowed the euphemistic name of dinner.' (*For other examples of British understatement see* Fraffly, Plea stretter *and* Retter-wesser).

Firs Chig Gerta: First you go to. As in: 'Firs chig gerta Mob Lodge'; 'Firs chig gerta Rich in Spock, theng ketcher choobor bus—cheffer zizzier'; or 'Firs chig gerta Girlda Skrin. Fay were ewered ketcher chewball chepp.'

Folker Swell: If the conditions are favourable. As in: 'Folker swell we shoopie thep-eye hops four'; or 'Aif put foddy thousand quid into Ruckluppalot Carpets. Ashel mecca pecket—folker swell.'

Forecourt Sec: Opinion differs widely as to the derivation and etymology of this term. Some authorities, because of the word 'sec' *(French:* dry), claim that it refers to the enclosure, or forecourt, in front of the private entrance to a castle, which was reserved for the use of visiting influential princes (VIPs), and that this was known as the dry enclosure, or *forecourt sec,* because it was considered inhospitable to pour molten lead over this area. Others, basing their claims on the historical evidence that there were no visiting princes who would have been improved by a little molten lead occasionally, say that it has nothing to do with enclosures or princes; and maintain that it is a corruption of *fog-caught sick,* meaning: sick while crossing the Channel. One distinguished philologist even goes so far as to say that it means: a surfeit of pea soup.

However, because of the context in which it is usually to be found, viz. in exclamations of impatience or anguish, the present writer's opinion is that these theories, although ingenious, are not seriously to be entertained; and that it is derived from the vaguely similar English expression: For God's sake! For example: 'Forecourt sec, Rawsmerreh! Hommny Thames dway heffter osk you to *shobben* this kovving naif?'

or: 'Forecourt sec, Darkless! One dar swish youder tlisspy sirius for a merment. Yorpa heffing lecker chailed.'

Fraffly: Frightfully. So much has been said and written in the past about British *under*statement that the equally widespread and equally characteristic British *over*statement is sometimes overlooked. The following examples, first of the former, then of the latter, are typical.

Understatement

THE SITUATION: Mr Smith arrives home to find his hall carpet badly mudstained by the men who came to put out the fire which has partially consumed his cottage after it had been accidentally set alight by the man who had just left, with Mrs Smith, for Paris. His comment: 'How tossum.'

THE SITUATION: A mad foreign major, somewhere east of Suez, has pressed a button which releases an intercontinental ballistic missile which falls on London, completely destroying the City and the Isle of Dogs. A flying fragment of masonry has fractured Mr Smith's left ankle, and his new suit is hanging in ribbons from his shoulders. Somewhere in the rubble, under the remains of his bowler hat, is his right ear. His comment: 'Relleh, these foreigners go a bit too far!'

Overstatement

THE SITUATION: Mr Smith, having miraculously recovered from the above disasters, except for the fact that he hasn't grown a new ear, enters a wine merchant's in the West End. After buying a bottle of sherry, he says, 'Thank you,' and is about to leave. The wine merchant says, 'Thairk yaw. Notter tolcer. Fraffly nacer few to bisso caned. Fraffly caned a fume shore.'

THE SITUATION: Mrs Smith, before leaving for Paris, peers accusingly at her reflection in the mirror. She notices a small pink-gin stain on the front of her frock. Her comment: 'My God, I look paw stiffleh *gosstleh*!'

THE SITUATION: An advertisement is to be prepared for a manufacturer of surgical appliances. The outcome: A headline which reads, 'Ruptured but on top of the world.'

Girril; Kell: Because of the context in which these words are to be found it is assumed that they both mean the same thing as the English word *girl*. The OED's first definition of *girl* is: *1. A child or young person of either sex.* This is preceded by a symbol which denotes that this definition is obsolete. The OED's second definition is: *2. A female child; applied to all unmarried women.* This is followed by the numerals 1530—the date of the earliest known occurrence of the word used in such a way as to allow this definition to be applied. Now if, until 1530, the same word was used to describe both boys and girls, it surely must have been because, until that date, it had been found impossible, or at least difficult, to tell which was which; or perhaps it was because no one had taken the trouble to investigate the matter.

Although the Gregorian calendar was not adopted in Britain until 1752, the ordinary, non-leap, 365-day year was officially introduced by Julius Caesar in 46 BC. So it would seem that this momentous year, 1530, was an ordinary, long sort of year such as we enjoy at the present time—365 days and 365 nights. A long time; it is a pity that the OED is not more specific. On what particular day or night during this long year was the important discovery made that boys are different from girls? Was it 2 February? 29 November? or what? And who made it?

If Pope Gregory XIII and Julius Caesar can get into the OED merely for the introduction of calendars (which anyone can get for nothing at Christmastime), surely the anonymous benefactor who invented sex should at least get a mention, even if his (or her, but most probably his) name is unknown. And where did this discovery, which must have radically altered the way of life of the British people, take place?

The OED says not a word. Only conjecture remains; and it falls upon the present writer to assume the role of conjecturer.

ACT I
Scene I

In the bathroom of the humble dwelling of Master John Bye, his wife, Mistress Mary, and their three girls, Joan, Rosalind and Richard. The date: 29 July 1530.

John Bye, a weaver by trade, has managed, by much skimping and saving, to afford a bathroom—an unheard-of luxury in those days. He had always wanted a bathroom, being of a contemplative and speculative turn of mind; and he knows that the best place to indulge in speculation is in the bath. This bathroom is, by twentieth-century standards, a primitive affair; a simple wattle and daub lean-to against the wall of the cottage, and entered by crawling through a two-foot-high aperture at floor level. The equipment comprises a wooden, coffin-shaped bath; a jar of sand and shavings with which John scrubs himself clean; an earthenware pitcher; and an enormous iron cauldron in which he heats up his bathwater over an open fire of wood, collected from the adjacent forest by his daughter Richard.

When the scene opens, John is lying in the bath, his left forefinger, as usual, in a knot-hole in the side of the bath. This is to prevent the water from escaping, for although inventive, and of more than normal intelligence, he hasn't yet got round to dreaming up what is now known as the 'plug'. He is staring moodily at the wall in front of him, frowning and lost in thought. He is also shivering, as he has been there for several hours and a thin film of ice has formed over the surface of the bath water. The end of his finger, protruding through the knot-hole, is a severe case of frost-bite. It is, after all, still only July in the little village of Grigglesmere, near London, in southern Britain.

Master John sneezes loudly, and blinks, for the first time for several minutes. The sneeze brings him back from the depths of thought in which he has for so long been submerged. He looks around him. Slowly his expression changes from one of rapt concentration to one of incredulity. Then a slow smile dawns, a smile which soon changes to a look of joy and elation. Suddenly, leaving his finger behind him in his excitement, he jumps from the bath and, without waiting to dry his wet and shivering form, dives through the hole in the wall into the next room.

John (*disappearing from view*): My goodness, MacInnes! One has found it!

Scene II

The room into which John now suddenly emerges. He scrambles to his feet and runs rapidly around the room in a clockwise direction. He eventually catches up with his wife, Mistress Mary, who has been running ahead of him in a desperate effort to avoid being trampled underfoot. He clasps her around the neck, and laughs with tears of joy.

John: Merreh, Merreh! One has found it! At lawce twon nirze the onser!

(*Note: It may be seen that even at this early date the outlines of what was later to be known as Fraffly were beginning to appear among the better educated and more fortunate. John had always been a bright lass, and the squire had taken an interest in his welfare. It was due to this contact with the Manor that John spoke in slightly more genteel tones than one would normally expect of a humble weaver.*)

Mary: Och, mon. (*Mary's father is a Scot.*) Is there to be no end to your shenanigan? (*Her mother is Irish.*) Oiby sproised ut thee. (*Her parents have a paying guest, a foreigner from Dorset, or Nottingham, or somewhere like that.*) Fairth, mon! Lookit ye wee finger. Oy mean lookit ye stoomp, lud. Eeeeee!

John: Merreh! One has jaw smedder merst emezzing discoffreh! One has jaw stedder rare flession! Some girrils are not girrils a tal, but something quett different. They're you nick. Quett you nick.

Mary: Och, lud, there ye go agin. Oiby buffled by sich woild unholy tok. What mean ye, John? Moy lussies are not lussies uff trol? Fairth, mon, ye'll droive me oop the wol with thy crairzy mix-top tok. (*She glances anxiously through the hole in the wall which serves as a window.*) Here, lud. Cover oop thy nekkidness, choom. The bailiff skoomin!

(*She hands him a large pewter spoon. Enter, the bailiff.*)

Bailiff: Nah then, nah then, woskoa nonnear? Warsaw lisserbaht?

Mary: Och, father, sir, mon. It's John agin. He's bin rare flating agin. The noo he's a-sayin' oiby not the mother of girls. Eeeee, father, Bailiff, sir. Mare the holy Saint Pathrick in his infinite moicy forgive him. Och, father, 'tis the end of the worrrrrrrld!

John: Demmer tol, Merreh, one dar swish you wouldn't carreh on so.

Bailiff: This is a serious allegation, John Bye. I must warn you that anything you say may be taken down… (*Mary starts to cry. The Bailiff turns towards her.*) Come, Mistress Mary, prithee allow an old chum to comfort thee. There, there, forsooth, there now. (*He pats her on the head.*) John, may I have a few words with you in private about this matter? Let us adjourn to yon bathchamber.

Exeunt John and Bailiff, on all fours. Mary continues to wring her hands, and snivel into her wimple.

Mary: Och, he'll be the death o' me. Where will it ol end? Fairth, oilby nothin' but silver threads among the gold afore the Holy Father's sweet dawn breaks. (*Curtain.*)

ACT II

Scene: The following afternoon, in the market place. The cobbled square is thronged with Grigmirrians in festive attire—for this is an important occasion. Every hundred years or so, whenever a discovery is made, or whenever a special announcement is to be made, such as notice of an increase of the tax on daub, the inhabitants hurry to the market place to hear what it's all about.

On a dais at one end of the square are grouped John and Mary, with Joan, Rosalind and Richard. The bailiff is also there, wearing an admiral's hat. Since we last saw Mary, time has wrought a miraculous change…she now looks happy, composed and stunned. The girls, except Richard, are smiling too. Only Richard looks a little apprehensive, and keeps muttering something about: Nonsense!

John carries his head high, and although making an effort to appear calm, cannot suppress his excitement. He knows, for the public to take his announcement seriously, he must cultivate an air of boredom and indifference—even stupidity. In an effort to hide his intelligence, he drools a little, lets his tongue hang out and squints inwardly towards an imaginary fly on the bridge of his nose. To emphasise his apparent idiocy, he addresses the bailiff as: Massa-sahib, sir. The bailiff beats on an empty mead bottle with a halberd to capture the attention of the crowd.

Bailiff: Ladies, may I have your attention please? Master John Bye, whom I have had the pleasure of knowing since he was a little girl, has an important announcement to make about another revelation.

Cheers and catcalls; shouts of 'Good old John,' 'No doubt about you, John,' and 'Prithee, what now, buster?' The bailiff holds up his hand for silence, and continues.

Bailiff: I ask you all to listen carefully to what John has to say, before you give vent to the complex emotions which his announcement will undoubtedly provoke. (*The crowd shuffle uneasily, and gaze at each in wonder. A little girl starts to cry.*) Here, now then, is our guest speaker, ladies! Master John Bye.

John (*rising to his feet and addressing the crowd*): May earl friends, femmay sokol you, one shell come stretter the point. No doubt you follwares thot of yourselves as girrils. Well, ladies, one has med the emezzing discoffreh that urnly abot hoffer few are girrils. Sholleh, at one taymore another, sommer few maif nerticed… (*He gradually expounds his hypothesis to the spellbound crowd. This is followed by detailed argument, illustrated by diagrams drawn on a slab of slate with a piece of chalk from a nearby quarry.*) And so, ladies (*he concludes*), that is that!

When he has finished there is complete silence. John looks anxiously at his audience. It is clear, from his expression, that he is wondering whether they will have him arrested, and perhaps hung, drawn and quartered—or even just quartered. They are talking among themselves in hushed tones. Then, at last (and John may be seen offering up a silent prayer of gratitude) what he has apparently been waiting for arrives—a quiet but unmistakable giggle! Then there is excited conversation,

*banter and scuffling. Finally, from somewhere in the crowd, comes the long shrill cry:
'Wheeeee!' The crowd rush to the dais, lift John and his family onto their shoulders,
and tramp off to the tavern, singing 'Freezer Chollicker Fairler'.*

ACT III

*Scene: The following day, inside the great hall of the Manor. John is wearing a mor-
tarboard made from old manuscripts, and a long gown of lambswool and feathers.
The squire is sitting at the table surrounded by his advisers. Attendants, wearing the
ridiculous clothes that young people once wore, are busy at their spinning wheels, or
mooching around doing nothing. Mary and the bailiff are curtseying to each other in
a corner. Solemnly tripping vergers, with short silver wands, play lutes and hautboys.
As the curtain rises, John is talking earnestly to the squire.*

John: …and so, with yorpa mission, square, one would lake to call
these girrils…I mean, thee screechers, after your good self. One sick-
shaw greshess permission to call them 'squares'. Pipple sholpy known
as 'squares and girrils'.

Mary: Och, squoire, father. It is a-wantin' oiby that they be called
after may darlin' hoosbund hisself. Fairth, father, oiby…

John: Will yupeh quiet, Merreh! His lottship campy bothered with
your drivel. Relleh, Merreh! Nir, 'squares and girrils'. Dern chewgree,
square?

*There is a long whispered conversation between the squire and his advisers.
Finally the squire speaks.*

Squire: Master John, this discoffreh of yoss is of sotcher megnitude
that it is urnly rate and propah that thee screechers shoopey nemmed
ofter your good self. They sholpy nirn as Byes! Ay heff sperken!

Mary (*jumping to her feet, and running from the fireplace, where she has been
praying noisily*): Mether good lord be prezzed. Och, father, squoire, sir.
Oiby hoy and droy in me deloight. They're to be called after me darling
hoosbund, John Boye! It's a Boye. It's a Boye. It's a Boye! (*Exit Mary,
squealing. Curtain.*)

*Dernchew filshie
pled the
Moonlet Snotter
quett
chommingleh?*

Wonker nurnleh
seth etta
Bok is
worse than
her Bare-turfen

Glare Twef: Glad to have. As in: 'Glare twef mare chew'; or 'Glare twef head the prearflitch.'

Gooner Skreshers: An exclamation of surprise, often followed by the words: 'Hoss choop toffmeh!'

Hammer Freddy: That elusive man who continually evades telephone conversations. His switchboard operator and his secretary have so effectively, and for so long, protected him from unwanted callers, and have so jealously guarded his privacy, that no one has ever spoken to him. In fact, it's doubtful if he even exists.

> Hammer Freddy's knotter term.
> Hammer Freddy isn't in.
> Hammer Freddy skonta Rirm;
> (A plester witchy sneffer bin).
>
> Hammer Freddy isn't heah.
> Hammer Freddy's in the bawth.
> Hammer Freddy's out, I feah;
> (Or leads you op the goddon pawth).
>
> Hammer Freddy's hirmin bed;
> Woo-choo kettering at four?
> Hammer Freddy may be dead.
> Hammer Freddy is no more.

Harsh Turns: A subdued voice. To 'spiggin harsh turns' means to speak in a whisper, or very quietly and respectfully, as one does in Wessmin Streppy, in churches, banks and other places of worship.

Hawk Raw Spons: Small, round, slightly sweetened raised cakes, marked with a cross, and eaten at Eastertime. In earlier times hawk raw spons contained fruit and spices. *Sometimes also known as:* Hock Response.

Holly Street: The street in London where doctors like to congregate. This street is not as famous as it used to be in the days before do-it-yourself medicine became so popular. Anyone, now, for the price of a paperback, can diagnose anything from leucoderma to leprosy. The magic phrase is *psychosomatic*, which means 'yours-mine'; i.e. '*I* have an interesting malfunction caused by a new and obscure virus; *you* have a defence mechanism, no doubt over-compensating for an Oedipal trauma.'

Hoss-womming Potty: A party taking place in a house or other dwelling to celebrate the incoming of new occupants; and in order to give the place a 'lived-in' appearance. The procedures adopted at hoss-womming potties may vary considerably, depending on the financial position of those attending. Usually the guests, who often appear without the prior knowledge of the occupants, bring with them the bottles of Cyprus sparkling sherry-type burgundy; and the host and hostess supply the new carpet over which it is poured. The guests then drink their host's scotch, and spread asparagus over the upholstery. The purpose of this ritual is to let your host know that you feel at ease in his presence. Occasionally, when a chair becomes dismembered, or a curtain catches fire, one may hear the token apology, 'Fraffly sorrair; fiffly clomsairf meh'; but this is said in a spirit of fun, and is not intended to be taken seriously. In fact, such a statement is really just an opportunity for another guest to slap the apologiser on the back with a handful of stuffed eggs (these are always provided) and to scream with happy laughter.

Hunts: (*Not to be confused with* hunting. *See* Love of Animals *under the heading* Lov.) Hunts are the terminal portion of the human *oms*. They are specially modified, by having fingers and thumbs, for *grosping*, and for wearing rings of *dammonds and droopies*. Many songs and poems have been written about hunts, including 'Pell Hunts Aloft' and 'Mimmeh, Your Tanny Hunts Are Quet Chilleh'. (*c.f. the Strine word* hens. *As in:* 'Fowlerie, your tiny hens are frozen.')

Isty Ah; Ear Stirrof Koss: These two phrases belong to the *placatory banalities* group, and their use is almost entirely restricted to conversations between husband and wife, and in situations such as the following:

Henry Makeready and his wife, Margaret, are sitting alone in their comfortable and elegant sitting room in Kozzon Street, W1. They are enjoying a quiet drink before dinner.

Henry, who is something in the Sittair, and a prominent member of the Effluent Society, is a handsome and well-preserved but not actually pickled man of about sixty-five. His wife, a few years younger, is in a comparable condition of non-disintegration. Henry, having been born in the right place, at the right time and to the right parents, is a wealthy man. His wife has a small private income of about £75,000 per annum. The scene, quite apart from the opulence in which they sit, is a comforting one. Henry and Margaret have been married for forty years; and the various thicks and thins (mostly thicks) through which they have jointly passed have served to bring them closer and closer together, and to bind them into a relationship of mutual trust, understanding, respect—and other things.

Henry (*puffing at his fiftieth cigar for the day*): Hmmmm.

Margaret: Henrair, one dar swish you'd smirker treffle less.

Henry: Isty Ah.

Margaret: Joss termny Skozz do you smirkner deh, Henrair?

Henry: Isty Ah.

Margaret: Henrair!

Henry: Isty Ah.

Margaret (*raising her voice slightly, so that the chandeliers tinkle gaily*): HENRAIR!

Henry: Hmmm? Ah? Eh?

York oz wetting,
Mr Grem,
en hirriossa
gozzen your
briff kess.
Shellay tellser
Hovvy a botcher
offer of hoffer
million?

Earce, thairk yaw.
Omis Britton,
the gill-tetched
mocket shows somma
nizziness; emma
fred emma sosku to
except a smoll
reduction
in cellarair

Margaret: Henrair, air do weir shooed listen to meh. *Skozz*, Henrair. Hermny *skozz* dew smirkner deh?

Henry: Con seck seckly. Bot torth rare, preps. Preps thrair.

Margaret: Henrair, one door swish shoed tretter smirk less. Sotch bixer gozz too. Shorred kompy good for one. Sholly wonken remembah what Chollz said a botcher hot.

Henry: Isty Ah. Ear stirrof koss.

Margaret: Henrair, prommer smair you'll tretter cotter donter tour deh. For messeck, Henrair. Will you prommer smair?

At the mention of the dreaded word 'prommer', Henry has closed his eyes, to hide the fact that they have started swishing again. Whenever his wife says 'prommer smair' Henry's eyes start swishing violently backwards and forwards—looking for the escape hatch.

Now, here they go again—swish, swish. His discomfort is acute; and, as torpor is the one thing he hates to be aroused from, when in his wife's presence, an immediate change of subject appears to be indicated.

Henry: Isty Ah. Of costier. Ah—beh the weh. One head loncheon with Sir Deffid todeh. Mersten choiple, relleh. Interesting chep. Stelling sobbott the tem; forry wosser Kuice-Air, of koss; forry took silk…Ah, hmm! Mersten choiple, mersten choiple.

Margaret: Henrair. One wishes you wouldn't chenge the *sopp*-checked.

Henry: Isty Ah. Costier. Emmest seh, Sir Deffid simster mitter binnex troddnerreh emmiable chep. Nor chong, of koss; bot nenty-fafferso. Bar—chuno; wonna vuss. Fay ness cheppin did.

Margaret: Henrair, sholleh yourra member what Chollz said a botcher hot.

Henry: Ears of costier. Hmmm. Yooster bin the Godze, of koss. Fother worrof koss. Twirld frection nowf koss.

Margaret: Henrair! Prommer smair.

Henry: Ear Smogret, of koss. (*He gets up from his chair, walks across to the table, reopens his eyes and pours himself another drink. He also surrepti-*

tiously takes four cigars from a box and puts them into his pocket. He walks casually towards the door.) Shompy long. (*Exit.*)

Klim: Variant of: Klin (clean). As in: Klim perrer feels; klim breaster fit; and klim biller felth.

Kobbon: Non-metallic element. Found in: chockol, dammonds and kobbon pepper.

Krimmin Shooker: (*Sometimes:* Shookren Krim). Cream and sugar. As in: 'Chew teg krimmin shooker?' and 'Nir thairk yaw, but maif some shookren krim?'

Lov: Love. This may be any of the following kinds, listed in order of importance: (1) Love of animals, e.g. oysters, smoked salmon, etc. Otters and seals are also loved, but only if between hard covers and illustrated. (2) Love of royalty. (3) Love of children. This is now so widespread and so uninhibited that it has become a national problem, and the Government decided (*The Times*, 22 July 1967) to introduce summer time five weeks earlier than usual in 1968, thus giving children going home from school an extra hour of daylight; it being at this period of the day that love of children reaches its greatest intensity. (4) Love of customers, expressed verbally as 'Faun three yeppence, love,' 'Nome sorry, love,' etc. (5) Love of, or devotion to, a particular cause, such as Learning; clear evidence of which may be seen in the popularity of crossword puzzles. (6 *et seq.*) Love of other things too numerous to mention, but including: Love of television; Love of very old actors and actresses; Love of horoscopes; Love of Oxford *or* Cambridge; Love of obsolete steam locomotives and disused canals. Last of all, there is Romantic Love, as immortalised in the novel *Ledder Chettler Sloffah*.

The first of these loves, Love of animals, is so overwhelming a passion that more must be said about it. Proof of it, in the form of heads and skins, may be seen over many a British mantelshelf and on many a

British floor. There are even cases of people having loved *live* animals. This, when one remembers how many Englishmen have been eaten by animals in various parts of the world, demonstrates the unselfish nature of this devotion.

Mac: A tent-like object into which sleeves have been inserted, and with a buttoned opening down the front; worn as a protection against rain. A description of this garment, although painful to both describer and reader, is essential for the sake of accuracy. It is, by international rainwear standards, very long; the sleeves are anachronistically raglan; the collar of military cut; the pockets, one on each side, have vertical slit openings and are voluminous enough to hold the usual selection of slim volumes and guidebooks without which the wearer, unable to read in the rain, would feel naked, lonely and ashamed. Its style is described as 'classic', this being a euphemism for 'as worn by the suffragettes'. The colour is excessively nondescript in hue, and usually light in tone, so that the Mac will quickly show the dirt it attracts; the consensus of opinion being that a Mac should always look a little *grubbeh*. In spite of the forbidding appearance it gives to the person it envelops, it is not difficult to buy. In fact, it is difficult to buy anything else; and the only way to get hold of a non-Mac is to follow the hypothetical example of Mrs Waddington who, accompanied by her husband, recently set off on such a mission.

'Ear smottom,' said the assistant, 'of koss. Hee-wee or, mottom.' After a swift flicker of the eye, to judge the correct size, she selected a coat from a row of apparently identical ones on a rack. Mrs Waddington tried it on and, bracing herself for the ordeal, looked at her reflection in the mirror. If what she saw there was anything like what her husband could see, as he stood there, ankle deep in carpet, watching her—and with his wife's dear, warm, friendly, comfortable, familiar, elegant, but unfortunately needing to be replaced, raincoat over his arm—Mrs Waddington gave no indication of it. She neither screamed nor laughed; she didn't burst into tears. The effect of the raincoat, or 'Mac' as her London friend Madeleine called these things, was to transform her into that same extraordinary creature who had already, in the four previous shops they had been to, stared back at her from the mirror with an expression of incredulity and loathing. Mrs Waddington was fairly tall; about five foot six. She had moderately square shoulders, and her neck was of no more than average length. The thing in the mirror looked like an eight-foot high gaberdine champagne bottle surrounded by a hostile knob three inches in diameter. 'Do you have anything else?' she asked the assistant. 'Something a little unusual, perhaps?'

A momentary look of anguish passed over the assistant's face. 'Ah *newshol*, mottom! But this is a *classic*, mottom. Ekna shaw yaw that choolpeh ebble to wear this in ten yah stame.' She made an adjustment to the collar, and stood back, her head on one side, looking at the result with approval.

'I'm afraid it's not quite what I'm looking for,' said Mrs Waddington, starting to remove the coat. 'I'd like something a little, well—a little shorter. This seems very long.' She turned to her husband. 'What do you think, John?'

'Beautiful material,' he replied, guardedly, trying to placate the assistant; he could see that she was a little upset by the word 'unusual'. 'No, really, dear, I don't think it suits you. Better to see if you can get something a bit, ah—smarter.'

'Well of koss we do huff tin-etchers' coat smottom. In the goddning depotment on the second floor. B'trelleh, mottom, thet co-chaw werring is a *classic*; it'll be jester smot in ten…' The inevitable 'yah stame' trailed away inaudibly. Something in Mrs Waddington's manner must have got through.

'What about some other sort of material?' Mrs Waddington asked.

'Oh *nir*, mottom. Nothing like that.' For the first time there was a hint of disapproval. She took the coat and replaced it on the hanger.

'Sorrair, mottom. Fred we corn telpew. Thairk yaw. G'doft noon, mottom.'

As they emerged into the street, Mrs Waddington said, 'What was that about the gardening department? Why would they have coats in the gardening department?'

'Oh, I don't know,' said her husband. 'They do that sort of thing.' He had had a similar experience the previous day when he had tried to buy a chopping board in the kitchenware department of a shop in Kensington. 'Had enough?' he asked.

'Let's try one more,' said Mrs Waddington.

'Okay,' he said. 'But they all look the same to me. I wonder why they make them so long? What about that first one we saw? At least it was blue. And only twenty-five guineas or something.' He was getting more and more tired. They hadn't seen anything that even remotely resembled the coat they were looking for, and which they had imag-ined would be so easily obtainable in this vast and fascinating city. Mrs Waddington had been told, 'Wait until you get to London; they have marvellous coats there.' Well, in a way, this was true.

'Perhaps,' said Mr Waddington, remembering the gardening de-partment, 'we've been going to the wrong shops. Do you think we ought to try a shoe shop? No, no, not a shoe shop,' he added quickly, remem-bering past experiences. 'Perhaps an outfitter's—whatever that may be. Or how about waiting until we get to Stockholm or somewhere?'

'Here we are, dear,' said his wife, and they entered the sixth shop.

Here, however, the same thing was repeated, except for one un-expected development. After Mrs Waddington had tried on several identical Macs, the assistant asked, 'What abot a kep, mottom? Hee-wee heff a relleh chomming kep. Wif had a lot of success with these.' She took the cape from its hanger and draped it over Mrs Waddington's passive shoulders, and fastened it at the neck. 'The odvontage of a kep, mottom, is that it's ollwares the sem; it'll be exactleh the sem in ten yah stame. Here, mottom, your roms go through these little holes—leck

We sother
bend of messed
papes on
Haw Skod Spread;
Bitting the
Ritritchu know

Essay, Mogret,
may ay heff one
of yossy grets?
Ay fleft
messy gretser
tome

thet; sir chooker new shore roms. Ay ollwares think a kep's a chollicker dead ear; and, of koss, it'll be the same in fifteen yah stame.'

So the ante had now been raised to fifteen years! Mr Waddington looked down at the floor, to avoid catching anyone's eye. The pale peach-coloured carpet, apparently laid over four inches of foam rubber, moved under him like junket, adding the symptom of nausea to his already overloaded syndrome. It was time to go into action.

He turned to the assistant, and with as amiable a smile as he could contrive, asked her if she had any longer capes. 'This one doesn't even touch the floor,' he said. 'And what about a matching helmet? Do you have any jolly helmets?'

'Nurma fred this is the urnly one we hev, sir. We follwares med them this ware.' She smiled at him indulgently. 'The helmets are on the gronflaw in the shoe depottment. '

As they were walking along Piccadilly in the rain, Mr Waddington stopped suddenly. 'Just a moment, dear. They're having a sale here. Look at those sweaters. Shetland. Only eighty-four shillings. That's very little. I need a sweater. Come on in.'

The shop, a small one, appeared to be selling its entire stock at less than half the marked prices. Shirts, in various stages of tiredness but briskly bizarre in colour, had been reduced to as low as fifteen shillings. Ties were going for practically nothing. Sweaters, jackets, coats—everything appeared, to Mr Waddington's experienced eye, to be of excellent quality and remarkably inexpensive. A rack of coats caught his eye.

'I could do with a new raincoat myself, now that I think of it,' he said, selecting a smart-looking three-quarter length, navy blue, belted one with a flamboyant red lining. He asked if he might try it on. It settled comfortably over his shoulders, and around the back of his neck, the way a well-cut coat always will. The pockets were in exactly the right place. There was even a little pocket within a pocket, for small change: something which he had always liked. The belt (he hadn't worn a belted coat for twenty years) made him feel young again.

His headache had vanished. 'How much?' he asked.

'Ettky nez,' said the man.

'Good. I'll take it.'

'Just a moment, dear,' said his wife. 'Do you mind if I try it on?'

When they left the shop a few minutes later, Mrs Waddington was wearing the short, smart, elegant, navy blue coat with the red lining, and Mr Waddington was carrying her old one in a large paper bag with a handle.

Mummeh and Daddeh: Mother and Father; the ultimate arbitrators of right and wrong. As in: 'Hammer Fred they're urnly cotton sheets, deah. Conta medgin what Mummeh would have said'; 'Daddeh ollwares wore hen mare chews'; or 'Mummeh and Daddeh yoosta seh there's nothing quettleck Spode.'

Nairflet–: (*Sometimes:* Yoom snairflet–). Prefix, corresponding to the English 'never let', to which various suffixes may be added, e.g. chaw; cham; sko; ter; tit; etc. As in: 'Nairfletchaw way-feet peas with a naif'; 'Nairfletchom mostosh be calm and tangled in the coffee grindah'; or 'Nairflettit be known the chorder monstrative, even about the British Bulldog, though the British Bulldog nairfletsko.'

Nannie: A female person, of any age, who looks after that particular order of children who remain at the perambulatory stage until they reach puberty. In backward countries it is not uncommon to see children as young as eight or nine years actually trotting along beside their parents, and using their feet; but not in the land of Nannies—here they remain perambulated until they start wearing bras and bowlers. On a fine Sunday morning in Hyde Park or Kensington Gardens (it doesn't have to be *too* fine), one may often see two Nannies talking together while the occupants of their prams engage in a serious discussion about polo, international affairs, or takeover bids. A reliable and efficient Nannie, or *treasure*, finds employment by answering advertisements such as the following, which appear in the 'personal' columns of newspapers.

> RESOURCEFUL, articulate and imaginative Nannie wanted for revolting children of intelligent and rapidly expanding company director and his terrifically attractive but brutally whimsical wife. Applications will be considered from those requiring a demanding and backbreaking position with fun-loving vegetarians. Knowledge of Spanish essential. Must be young in spirit and have own mini or scooter.

Nems: Names. As the pronunciation of British family and place names, e.g. Cholmondeley, Cirencester, Featherstonehaugh, etc. has already received more than adequate coverage by other authorities, mention is made here only of those few more familiar Christian names which appear to have escaped attention.

Men: Author, Claif, Darkless, Deffid, Filks, Gems (or Chems), Goddon, Grairgrair, Grem, Jodge, Moggon, Otchbolled, Pol, Salmon, Tawneh, Undraw, Wretch.

Women: Airmlair, Blondge, Ed-led, Fibbie, Frondses, Hillrair, Idith, Jawjar, Jossfin, Lairslair, Mebble, Medlen, Merreh, Mogret, Mosha, Proonce, Vellrair.

No Hommentreng: The practice of attempting something which one knows to be impossible, and which may have disastrous consequences for other people, but not for oneself because one has been prudent enough to have an escape route or face-saver already planned. As in: 'Koss wonkered bomb the Embassy *and* send a peace feeler. Nommer choper koss. Still—no hommentreng.' (*See also* Potty Poltix.)

Offkosser: Of course, sir. This curious word, terminating in what is known as the *ritualistic suffix*, is one of many such terms, e.g. notter tolcer, quettser, retter-wesser (*q.v.*), surn lisser, yesser, etc. These have survived from the days when the use of the word 'sir' signified respect for someone who was socially superior to, or richer than, oneself. It has no such significance today. In the democratic British society where, socially and financially, all people are equal, its continued use is an anachronism. It now signifies either nothing at all, or mild scorn. As in: 'Offkosser, if you dern't *want* the roomser, youk nollwares vairkettitser. Off trolcer, wiffer nan norma sweating list. G'monningser.'

One: Fraffly, as pointed out elsewhere (*see* Orstrellion) contains many English words, of which 'one' is one. In both languages 'one' is a number, a single unit corresponding to the symbol 1. In Fraffly, however, 'one' is also the first-person singular pronoun 'I'. In Fraffly one says not I but one, even though this may sometimes result in something that sounds like nonsense, like: 'One thought one had won one, and one had won one, too.' Ordinarily, however, the meaning is clear enough, e.g. 'One knows when one zop stezz'; or 'One was jolleh depressed.'

Orstrellion: Of Australia or its inhabitants; Strine. The Fraffly and Strine languages are similar in some ways, both being derived from a common source—English. Many Fraffly, English and Strine words are identical, and have identical meanings. These are mostly short words such as: he, she; it; for; from; to; at; etc. The student will soon discover, however, that many words, although identical in spelling and phonetically, are otherwise unrelated. A word may have a different meaning in each language. Take, for example, the word 'chair' (plural: chairs) which has the following three different meanings.

English: Chair: A seat, usually for one person, movable, with four legs and a back, and it may have arms. As in: 'I sit on my chair all day and pray that the band'll play in Mandalay'; or 'Her eyes flew to the chair and rested there for a few seconds.'

Fraffly: Chair: A shout, or acclamation of joy, applause, etc. As in: 'Three hoddy Brish chairs'; or 'Chair op, Cholleh, you'll soompy dead.'

Strine: Chair: A boy's or man's name. As in: Chair congeal went up the hill; Chair canner beanstalk; for yicken sigh Chair Krobinson, etc.

The differences between Fraffly and Strine, however, are more marked than the similarities. This may be seen from the following poem, from *Kangaroo Valley, SW5,* by Ida Nohoo.

> 'Assay,' ass said, 'her Fraffly caned
> A few to bisso ness.
> Orstrellion, preps?' ass said. 'Ay faned
> You heffnor Strellion fess.'
>
> But his replay war snoff reclair;
> He said, 'My ficer smine.
> Nair, nickor fang gedadda vere;
> You mice tart torgon Strine.'

Plea Stretter: This violently obscene oath is used only under extreme provocation, as when some great physical pain can no longer be borne, or when a number of exasperations combine to create a state of anguish which can no longer be contained by normal stiffupperlippery.

Example I: Mr Anderson is lying quietly on his back lawn in the sun. It is late Sunday morning, and he has not yet recovered from a party which his friends inflicted on him the previous night, and at which, because he has been desperately worried about a rumour which he heard in reference to his wife and a neighbour, he had far too much to drink. His eyes are covered over by a black scarf, to keep out the glare; and he is trying, by thinking about the cigarette burns on the piano, to forget the condition of his new carpets. He is also suffering from piles. The undercarriage from a carelessly assembled aircraft flying overhead falls into his garden, severs his left leg two inches below the knee, and overturns his glass, which had been still half full. He removes the scarf from his eyes, looks towards the disappearing aircraft, and says, 'Plea stretter be a *little* more kefful.' His wife, hearing the commotion, rushes out and asks, 'My God, George, what happened?' George, having by now regained his composure, replies, 'Fellow knocked my dring curver.'

Example II: Mr Hawkins, a senior account executive in a large advertising agency, is sitting at his desk with his head in his hands, and with the door locked. He has just had a telephone call, telling him that *the* client, *his* client, the one who brings three-quarters of a million pounds into the agency each year, has transferred his affections elsewhere. On Mr Hawkins's desk are two letters. The first is from an insurance company, telling him that, as the policy hadn't been renewed, his country cottage, recently destroyed by fire, is a total loss. The other letter is a threatening one from his secretary's fiance, concerning a matter of attempted rape. The seventh sonic boom for the day has just passed. Suddenly there is a loud explosion (something to do with gas mains) in the street immediately outside what had until then been his window. The entire ground floor is blasted in, and Mr Hawkins is covered by debris and broken glass. He notices, as he gets to his feet, that his new car, outside, is on fire. He goes to the place where the window used to be and, because he attempts to lean on a window sill which is no longer there, falls headlong into the street. As he falls, he says, 'Will you plea stretter meg a *little* less noise?'

Poncer: Pardon, sir. As in: 'Ah peck your poncer, but mairn tropp choofra merment?'

Potty Poltix: A game, thought by some to be played at the Hosser Commons, but actually played in corridors. It is a difficult game, combining techniques derived from such varied sources as chess, karate, the professional stage, tightrope walking and 'no hommentreng' (*q.v.*).

Retter-wesser: Rightaway, sir. This typical example of British understatement means: 'I shall attend to it in my own good time. I shall go now and not return for several days, during which time I shall be concerned only with my own affairs; and if you think I'm going to wait hand and foot on you, you fat slob, you can think again. One of these days, when I have found a better job, I shall not only tell you exactly what everyone thinks of you, but shall also probably cause you to become disembowelled.'

It will be seen that British understatement is a most valuable weapon in the battle to survive in an increasingly complex technological society. Not only does it act as a soothing lubricant, preventing all friction; it also saves a lot of time, and reduces the cost of telegrams. For example, 'Four cases despatched last Friday' is universally understood to mean: 'Owing to the fact that no one in the organisation is prepared to authorise the renewal of the tea urn, the men are out on strike. We haven't even started work on your order, much less packed the bloody stuff. Also, our sub-contractors have let us down badly; the telephone has been disconnected because we haven't paid the long-overdue account; and the managing director's secretary left suddenly yesterday for reasons which needn't concern you. It will probably be weeks before we despatch your order, and we are hoping that you will spend the intervening time in an exchange of correspondence with the British Railways.'

Rest Raw: (*Sometimes:* Rare Straw). A public eating house, where raw food rests for a few days before being flavoured with rare straw. Any mention of Fraffly rest raws would be incomplete without a few words about decor. Although the food in most rest raws is identical (being piped underground, one understands, from a central depot on the outskirts of London); and although the rituals which accompany its delivery to the customer vary but little, the decorations exemplify the extraordinary and limitless creative imagination of the British designer. (*See also* Connor Bess Street.)

Chollson air
thinking of
Pot-jiggle
this year,
or prep Spen.
Few binter
Spen lettleh?

**Josket beck.
Yoosht gerta
the You-netted
Stets.
Ay fon ditta
mirster musing
little pless**

Frustrated in many fields of endeavour by the limitations imposed by public taste and by modern production techniques, and hemmed in, until recently, by rigid censorship laws, the creative artist in Britain has had little opportunity to display his or her diverse and unique talents. However, in the ephemeral world of fashion, in rest raw decoration and in Connor Bess Street, it's an open slather.

To mention any particular establishment would, in view of the above definition of 'rest raw', obviously place the writer in a vulnerable legal position. The reader will, therefore, have to take his word for it. And his word? 'Man, the sky's the limit!' London rest raw decoration is as witty and exciting as it is varied; and, as it diverts attention from the food, satisfyingly functional.

Revving: Talking as though in a delirium. As in: 'Miss Jenny is a revving beauty,' meaning that she is beautiful but mad. As 'revving' also means 'revolving', it could mean that she is 'off her rocker and rolling'. Perhaps it means 'mad spinning Jenny'.

Sawnic Boom: Sound and shock waves produced by aircraft flying at a speed greater than that of sound, in order to shatter windows, windscreens and miscellaneous bijouterie, and in order to encourage the more widespread use of the telephone.

Shompy: Shall not be. As in: 'Shompy long. Beckon a few mints'; 'Shompy a tols praised'; or 'Shompy mourn a few wicks.' In Fraffly, the use of 'shompy' for the second and third persons, when the tense is future and the mood indicative, is grammatically correct. The archaic 'wopeh' although not incorrect, is seldom heard, and is considered pedantic; e.g. 'Once purses yaw shompy thah'—not: '…you wopeh thah.' It is interesting to note that the Strine word for 'shompy' is *wopey*, so similar to 'wopeh' that it is assumed to have been derived from it; e.g. 'I fedder gota bedfer a fued-eyes; so I wopey gona Airdelight till Money or Chewsdy.'

Sir Fiffly and Sir Offly Sorrair: Two gentlemen of leisure, brothers, who lived in Belgrave Square during the latter half of the last century; famous for their extraordinary politeness and outstandingly gentle manners. So polite were they that it was not uncommon, if they should arrive simultaneously at the entrance to their club, for each to insist that the other enter before him, and each to say, 'No, no, offter yaw,' for so long that they would both drop off to sleep, or icicles would form on them, so that they would have to be towed away and thawed. It is not very surprising then, even in London where the people are the most polite in the world, that the names of the Sorrair brothers should still be remembered, and used as expressions of apology for any minor breach of manners, or for some accidental clumsiness which has caused inconvenience or discomfort. Londoners are so polite that occasionally, when someone has trodden on your toe, or dislodged your eye with an umbrella, he or she will say, 'Fiffly Sorrair' or 'Sir Fraffly Sorrair' even a moment *before* the toe is trodden on or the eye dislodged.

Snorkner: It is not going to. As in: 'Snorkner beer noffter fillet'; 'Snorkner wren off trol'; or 'Snorkner megny difference.' 'Snorkner' appears to have been derived from the American *snart garnerby*, which is often heard in pronouncements such as: 'Armer talon new, Sheriff, this guy snart garnerby elected tamara; he's garnerby hengin frummer cartonwood tree.'

Sot Retchers: An expression of indignation. As in: 'One hears that we are soon twef decimal currency. Sot retchers! Ashel retteletter to the Thames'; or 'Look at that kel slegs! Sot retchers!'

Sottchen Metcher: Non-commissioned officer of the highest grade, and the target of many wry jokes. (*See also* Sawnic Boom.)

Sozz: A fluid dressing accompanying food. There is an old Fraffly saying, 'What's sozz for the goose is sozz for the mousse,' born of the belief that one should not enjoy food (*See also* Yoffa Bittna); and that exotic foods are oily, or too highly spiced. Sozz is made of flour, flavoured with the rare straw from which the English word *restaurant* is derived, and is much the same whether served with goose or mousse. Note: It is uncertain whether 'mousse' comes from *couvert de mousse* (*French:* moss-grown); from the verb *mousser* (*Fr. colloq:* to make angry); or is simply what it says—*mousse* (*Fr:* scum, foam, lather). Perhaps it is a combination of all three.

Spinnagret: It has been a great. As in: Spinnagret plesher; spinnagret prifflitch; spinnagret convinnience, etc.

Steffchaw: A kind of porcelain or earthenware, usually found in the form of a pair of symmetrically opposed, orange-ochre greyhounds, each reclining on a blue base on which also lies what is presumably the remains of a hare. The chief characteristic of Steffchaw is its capacity to generate in the beholder an overwhelming conviction that it is British and late eighteenth century in origin. Although widely distributed throughout the West End, and in spite of the discreetly unmangled appearance of the hare, Steffchaw rarely changes hands. The following ritual, with minor local variations, accompanies the non-sale:

Customer: Thet little dog yaw heaven the window. Thet Steff-chaw?
Dealer: Airk-chelleh, one rother fancies it surl yaw. Core swan compy shore.
Customer: Mare one see it?
Dealer: Of koss.

The dealer reluctantly extracts the piece from the window, in which are also displayed seven copper hunting horns; five decanters to which, over the small flaws in the glass, have been applied small 'price' labels, bearing such cryptograms as W/f4/Go9 *or* X/ff/aJ6; *eleven plates from a dinner service which once belonged to the King of Somewhere; a number of small silver and wooden boxes; a china mug, eighteen inches high and decorated with a transfer of Brighton Pier; seven ovoid Victorian alabaster hand coolers made last week in Italy; and other miscellaneous antiques.*

Customer: Looks fay lake Steffchaw. Mare nir the price?

Dealer: Freddit snoffer sell.

Customer: Er! Essie! Thairk yaw. G'morning. (*Exit—with some difficulty, owing to the presence of a large ginger cat sleeping in the doorway and a breastplate of Japanese armour looming overhead.*)

The establishments where Steffchaw is to be found are called 'Antiques', an American word meaning 'things made before 1939, and of any material except plastic and stainless steel'. The size, atmosphere and methods of display vary greatly. The 'antiques' may be one of a long row of little shops in Warport Road, or a spacious and elegant one near Shepp Smogged. It may be sandwiched in between a laundrette and a travel agent in a suburban street, or be a stall in a market.

The degree of specialisation also varies. The exhibits may, perhaps, be nearly all clocks or celestial globes, or Chinese porcelain and silver stirrup cups, or anything at all so long as there are two of them and facing in opposite directions. On the other hand, the collection may comprise every imaginable kind of flotsam swept in on the tide of dispossessed stately and non-stately homes, including such items as a miniature zither made of mother-of-pearl, a Georgian door key priced at £4, or an earthenware ginger-beer bottle. The proprietors come in as wide a variety of shapes and sizes as the goods they display—an elderly man who sits reading all the time and who knows the origin and history of everything in his shop, or a young girl proud of her complete ignorance.

Almost anything can happen in 'antiques'. An apparently new copy of a recent novel may have between its pages a pre-war 1½d bus ticket. You may, perhaps, find a small, cylindrical ivory 'thing', with screwed ends through each of which has been bored a neat hole, and marked 35/–. On being asked what it is, the proprietor may say, 'One doesn't know, but one hopes that one day someone will come in and tell one.' Or you may buy, for five shillings, a small mirror marked 25/–, and discover later, when you have recovered your senses, that it is so convex that you can see the moon in it, or so concave that what others might think is a speck of dust on your face is now seen to be a large cyst requiring immediate excision.

In some of the smaller shops it would be impossible to buy anything, even if the proprietor wanted to sell it, because the place is so congested that no one, not even an American, could get his hand into his pocket.

Stiffupperlippery: The British Stiff Upper Lip (*Labium rigidus britannicus*), introduced by Cromwell in 1653, has, with the passage of time, become a national symbol, loved and respected no less than Royalty, Shakespeare, Gad and, until recently, Sterling.

Stiff Upper Lips are to be found in front of every British hearth and telly; in every domestic, commercial, military and political situation. They have, for many years, been manufactured in plastic and exported, in times of crisis, to expatriate Englishmen in various troubled areas of the world. There was even a move recently to have a small Stiff Upper Lip, rampant, incorporated into the centre of the Union Jack, but unfortunately this project had to be abandoned because of the Lip's lack of satisfactory pictorial qualities. However, there is no doubt that, like sex and income tax, the BSUL is here to stay.

> Wender zoster urver teck shoe
> Never show it, though it breck shoe.
> In a crisis trooleh crooshol
> Wommer skerry honour shooshol.
>
> If the cheppsol ronju panic
> Beeder pressive—never manic.
> Though yorrode be steepen slippery
> Colter vet stiffupperlippery.

Sholleh you
compy sirius.
Shears a fess
lecker bet lex,
end four thombs.
Ay fender
paw stiffleh
noss yetting

Meddier boy,
youm snofferget
her femmlair
are Bocksher
people,
enchies fraffly
clefferetter
renching flozz

Prepshaw bitten by a shark;
Prepshaw boyza copper snark;
Prepshaw your dotter's rusticated,
Oversexed and undermated;

Prepshaw wife, olthoa buvver
Station, has a Latin lover;
Prepshaw floss-chaw job; have rebbies;
Fothered foreign-looking bebbies.

Catastrophic misadventures?
Clenchaw fistaw gritchaw denchers.
Jospie comm—and jospie static.
Dozen dooter beedra matic.

When the skyber ginster redden
At the dawna Vommageddon,
If a fellamex a fuss
Heedger sizzen wonna vuss.

Sweller's Bing: As well as being. As in: 'Sweller's bing a memmerer pollerment, zolso a fay keen burr twotchah'; or 'Sweller's bing a jol-lickered spot, yolso plessy organ.'

Tegger Topwith: Bring it to the notice of. As in: 'Ashel tegger top-with Thompson a midget lair'; or 'Ashered tegger topwith Sir Chems. Off trollits nockom plittleh—well, you knurlmen. Off trol tissabit are newshol.'

Temtebble: A tabular statement of the times at which events, e.g. departures and arrivals of trains and buses, sometimes take place. The compilation of these documents is determined entirely by the *twin prin-*

ciples of non-interference with personal liberty and minding one's own business so thoroughly that the smooth interconnection of different transport systems becomes impossible.

Over the centuries the British people have fought many battles for the liberties they now enjoy. One such battle, still being fought, is the battle against bureaucracy, and particularly against those bureaucrats who would like to see the synchronisation of train and bus departures and arrivals. There is every indication that the battle is nearly over; and that the bureaucrats have lost. Only in such a democratic nation as Britain, with each person jealously guarding his hard-won privileges, could such a victory be won.

The Thames: Well-known London newspaper, and the river after which it is named.

Thorcher mare: Thought you may. As in: 'Thorcher mare ketter tray woncer'; or 'Thorcher mare torcher your daughter, but orcher to torcher her in the orchard?'

Tin Etcher: A young person (specifically, aged thirteen to nineteen years) of either sex, whose clothes, habits and attitudes to life are a constant source of anxiety and criticism to those who are thirty or more years older and wish they weren't.

Toon Form Seppneh: One of the many terms relating to the strange and archaic currency system still in use in Britain. The English *pound* is divided into twenty *shillings*, each of which is divided into twelve *pennies* or *pence*. The resulting combinations of these oddities seem endless, e.g. thrin form seppneh; sefner nairpence; three yeppence; sempen seppneh; tum seppneh; tenner neat pants; faun formps; nen tinnen toppen seppneh; etc. Even: tookey nez; forky nez; tenky nez. A *guinea*, the unminted equivalent of twenty-one shillings, is known as wonky nair.

In spite of the many terms for individual sums of money, there seems to be no Fraffly collective name for money itself; presumably because it is so rarely mentioned, except in the privacy of the boudoir, the bank, or the broker's office. Everybody has money, of course, lots of it, but it is considered vulgar to display the fact. We all know these things exist, but there is no need to talk about them. Literature is as full of euphemisms for money as it is of those for other bodily necessities. A packet, or scads, or wads of boodle, brass, lolly, shekels, or spondulics—these are permissible; but not money. After all, the acquisition of money is a duty rather than a pleasure; and one doesn't like to brag about having done one's duty.

Though quite well off, *(a millionaire)*
I envy *(when I've time to spare)*
The other fellow; *(in the mob)*
So gainfully employed. *(with job.)*

Of course, an income, *(lots of dough)*
One is inclined to think, *(I know)*
Creates prosperity, employment.
(Gives me, my wife and friends enjoyment.)

For one's cigars; *(two quid; Havana)*
One's place in Berkshire; *(Tudor manor)*
One's food and drink; *(high-protein; bubbly)*
One pays one's tax. *(So thank me doubly.)*

This surely means: *(my broker tells me)*
The more I have, *(the more he sells me)*
The better off *(Oh, lucky me!)*
The nation *(that is, I)* will be.

So though, 'Uneasy lies the head
That wears the crown', as Shakespeare said,
One sleeps at night with conscience clear.
(And all those dividends each year.)

Ummint Sair: I mean to say. As in: 'Ummint sair; sol farewell nol thet; b'toff trol; ummin uno; ummin off trol sol farewell buttermint-sair...'

This incomprehensible statement, with arbitrary regrouping of individual phrases, may be continued and repeated for as long as several minutes. Its function is not to impart information, but to give the speaker time to devise evasive action in the face of an inconvenient question; or else to give the impression that one is stupid, as overt intelligence is often regarded as vulgar, like wearing clean gloves or saying 'I' instead of 'one'.

If the monologue is to continue for longer than about three minutes, it is considered advisable, in order to retain the listener's interest, occasionally to insert what are known as *condimental words*, or phrases, such as *you* or *your husband* (or any other subject in which the listener is interested—even *money*). These add pungency to a speech which might otherwise induce somnolence.

Vasseversa: Literally, one who writes poetry, or verse, while in gaol, or in a state of vassalage or servitude. Verse, or anything else, written under such unfavourable conditions, often reflects a distorted attitude to life, and so this word has gradually come to be applied to anyone who holds opinions differing widely from the prevailing ones, i.e. different from one's own. It is often used to describe prime ministers, mothers-in-law, schoolteachers, employers and employees. In English it has been corrupted to *vice versa*, meaning the transposition of the order of two things.

A manuscript found recently among the records of the church at the little village of Whistlestop, Hants, is a particularly fine example of the work of a vasseversa. It was written by Nicholas Nobbler, a glass painter who, in the fifteenth century, was incarcerated in the local oubliette for having given one of the deerhounds in his charge a shot of digitalis or, as it was then called, 'a smattering of ye foxglove'. This short poem, addressed to his gaoler, has been translated into modern language for the benefit of the reader.

> Dear Gaoler: Though this dungeon's cold and dank, you
> Must not think that I'm a moaner or a curser.
> For the treatment I've received, I hereby thank you
> From the bottom of my heart—and vice versa.

War Snebble: Was not able. As in: War snebble to mecket. Related phrases include: hoozar nebble; shomp yebble; quettar nebble; ear snebble; probblier nebble; werp yebble; nought shorrivizebble; and sensi skaned regodze but regretzy czar nebble.

Wren: Water falling in drops condensed from vapour in the atmosphere. As in: 'Look spit leg wren.' Wren may be in the form of intermittent 'sketted shozz', or it may be a 'nepsloot dompor'. If the former, it is ignored; if the latter, one goes for a walk in it, wearing Wellingtons and a Mac (*q.v.*). During the winter one always carries an umbrella, wren or shine.

Dome Billette

> You'll mishaw trendier; you'll billette.
> Oh, Gems, it look sleg wren.
> Your mac, dear, so you shonker twet.
> Don't liffer tin the tren.

> Ay thott, tonate, widdef thet biff.
> Sholl youpeh hirm bay four?
> Oh, ashu go, prep sugared leaf
> The garrodge dorra jaw.

Quetternay stog
enna fay good
femmlair,
but hoddlier
sootable
compenion,
fewnoa temmene

Egg-wetter gree.

Hiss fay

tossum.

Shell we tray

Grim Pok?

An Gems? A fyoolpeh nirra shop,
Sair Fottnoms, orra Tarrots,
Prep shoe would bisso kendenstop
And bayer boncher carrots.

Ethink we yolsaw nidder kess
Of something fother cellah.
Your brolleh, Gems! Oh, thidders cress
Of bing withoddonom brellah.

An heewee oddier, hishaw hat;
All hirriaw monning peppers.
Oh! Stoppit, Gems! You condu that
In fronder fol the neppers.

Yoffa Bittna; Yonnods Purster; Yoomce: Because of their close sociological interrelationship, it has been found convenient to group these three terms together. Each is admonitory; the first two, negatively (*English:* You are forbidden to; You are not supposed to); the last, positively (You must). They refer to the various laws and taboos which govern the lives of the British people, who are as law-abiding as they are polite and gentle mannered. Whether the continual use of these expressions is the result or the cause of the prevailing attitude to the law and to existing social conventions it is impossible to know, but their use is so widespread, and their effects so powerful, that one must regard them as symbols of the *Fraffly Ware Flafe*. The following examples are typical.

'Yoffa bittna feed cigarettes to thidge roffs, otter the otters'; 'Yonnods purster say *house*; yoomce toll wares say *cottage*'; 'Yoomce tollwares steng clirra the gets.' Occasionally 'Yoffa bittna' is replaced by the euphemism 'Please do not'. As in: 'These chihuahuas are fellyobble. Please do not inhale the exhibits.'

Yoomce nairflet choffrends hear you speaking English.
Speak Fraffly, though you mare not lake the words;
A newlpeh in your rateful pless,
The Opper Crossed! Dillateful pless.
Queen's English? No! That's strictleh fother birds.

FRAFFLY SUITE

FRAFFLY SUITE

Not Just a Language
But a Ware Flafe

Afferbeck Lauder

*Professor of Strine Studies,
University of Sinny;*

*Fellow of the Yarnurdov Foundation,
London*

Illustrated by *Al Terego*

Contents

Acknowledgments

The author expresses his grateful thanks to the people of London, particularly those in W1. Without them this book would never have been written.

He also expresses his warmest thanks to P. W. for his invaluable advice; to Mr Alistair Morrison for his, also; to Al Terego for his most perceptive drawings; and to the editor of *Prolix*, Mr Bruce Ampersand, for something or other, the author forgets what.

This work is fiction and the characters are imaginary.
Any likeness to persons, living, dead, or not yet born
(see pages 193–196) is purely coincidental.

Foreword

Professor Afferbeck Lauder, in his previous work, *Fraffly Well Spoken*, published last year, proved conclusively that here in London we speak a language called *Fraffly*, and not English, as we had always believed. This followed the earlier discovery of *Strine*, the language of Australia. Professor Lauder has thus established the general principle that every country has two languages, the official, written one, and the unofficial, spoken one. Now this is a linguistic, indeed an anthropological, breakthrough of considerable magnitude. Consequently, the publication of this new work by the professor is an event which seems to call for special recognition; something more than the usual summary reports in the learned philological journals. And so I decided to ask Mr Alistair Morrison, of Sydney, who has known Professor Lauder for many years, to seek an interview with him, for publication in the Jubilee number of *Prolix* which is soon to be issued to commemorate the first half-year of its existence. Mr Morrison agreed, and a report of what occurred appears below.

B. Ampersand
Editor, Prolix, London

Scene: A room in the Yarnurdov Foundation, in Boggly Square, London. Professor Lauder is sitting at his desk, surrounded by the usual professorial accoutrements and paraphernalia, including an eighteenth-century terrestrial globe and a pair of ormolu dividers, Roget's Thesaurus, a paste-pot and a curious pair of illustrated scissors from Japan, a bottle of benzedrene, an adding machine and a slide rule (for calculating royalties), and a half-eaten corned beef and pickle sandwich. Partially obscuring the William Morris wallpaper are framed, signed photographs of such notable people as Pola Negri, Max Beerbohm, Rutherford (Ernest, not Margaret), Lord Kitchener, Tiny Tim, and Billies Bunter and Graham. Over the mantelshelf, beside the stuffed head of a pale balding lexicographer (shot by Professor Lauder when on safari at Manchester University in 1947), hangs a portrait of H. W. Fowler, with a candle burning in front of it. The atmosphere is permeated by the odour of bibliolatry and Bach. The time is 3.30 pm. There is a knock at the door.

Lauder: Dooker min. (*Enter: Alistair Morrison, accompanied by—or, rather, held firmly in a half-nelson by—Mrs Crone, a grim and ancient majorette-domo who hoovers the professor's Bokhara, dusts his artefacts and brings him occasional plates of tepid mushroom soup.*)

Mrs Crone: Caught him red-handed, sir. Found him lurking, sir. Shall I call the police, sir?

Lauder: No, no, Mrs Crone. Let the man go, and please bring us some tea. (*Exit: Mrs Crone, mumbling. Professor Lauder turns to his visitor.*) Hot-ear do? Dr Livingstone, I presume.

Morrison: Hair yeggowan mite? Long time no see.

Lauder: Nwockernair doof yaw? Mayor yosk yon em?

Morrison: Morrison. Fom Sydney. Hacker chufa get?

Lauder (*peering over the top of his glasses*): Freffen seck! Off trolleys years.

Morrison: Lisser Nafferbeck, stop clowning an jar stenser a few questions. *Prolix* wantser ninterview.

Lauder: Earce, earce of coss. Weshel we stot? Whesher tepra cotta?

Bar chorleh
a smol gront from
the yacht skonsol
snommotch twosk for.

Sair
fotteh thozzen dosso.

Snommotch rilleh
when wonken sidders
the velue wov
wan swirker nolthet

Listen to mih, Deffid.
Ash leffer few words
with Sir Chollz.

Youm slifter mih.

Omshore wicken
compter somma
renchment.

Off trol Sir Choll
zizzer fairkered
frenter fozz.

Ollware cesspin

Morrison: Teller spatcher new book, Afferbeck. What's it called?

Lauder: *Notchester*.

Morrison: *Notchester*?

Lauder: Earce. *Notchester Lenguage But a Ware Flafe*. Nir, nir, thet's the sop-tettle. Scald *Fraffly Suite*.

Morrison: A nwotser taller bat? Howcha come to write it? I mean, well, now you take my case. You know the larsper kyrote, about... chew muster freddit, *Dubloms and Herrigotze*? Well it starts off with these two feller skoa nonner tripper rand Australia in a jeep. An wennay get to—

Lauder: Square teasie reading, rilleh. Not too technical. Written for the intelligent lemon, few noah temmean. Air-niffay do sesso mesself, I rother—

Morrison: Cairns. Way up in North Queen slant, Juno. Well they mee tupper this bird called Gloria, who runs a nespy book frorla cane-cutters. Cor say dono hooshie ears. Anyway, by this time she wonster gedadda Cairns. Sicker vorla cane-cutters an the grog-gernonner norl. Soshie hop zinner jeep wennair not lookin, annay carger tridderver. Well, one night there's a storm and—

Lauder: do feel thet this tem ev pulled it off. Baw tewsha leffer coppeh. Sefia self. (*He produces a slim volume inscribed 'To my very dear friend and colleague' and hands it to Morrison, who puts it in his pocket without looking at it.*)

Morrison: this Gloria dame, welshie sket stiffer lightning. Soshie creep zinter the tent where Norm and Reg are flake doubt after digger norlem po stoles, enchie creep zupter Norm, who spitfer no-hoper ree-ley, enchie cesstwim, Normshie says, Norm, wye carp! Anna neck-sing you know Norm scraplin wither. Knee says—

Lauder: Core swan dossen want to displeh wan's erudition too wop-fiercely, but wan mar stolso kippin maned wan skolligs. Rother a delicate bellence. Ha-wephyr, without, wan herps, seckrificing wan cinter lectual integriteh, wan doss feel wan hesstrock execkleh the—

Morrison: Hair, chuka tin-ear, Gloria, re says. Thaw chewer zinner jeepy says. Listen lovey says, dough wye car predge. Hair bat chewer nigh nicker norfa naffner bitter fun, lovey says. An Gloria, who zonner may kenniway, cesstwim, Normshie says, a mawl forrit. Weltercutter—

Lauder: rate nirt. There are ten chepters, a nimper twin are shot perms. Bare dopting this method, warner zebble to kill two birds with wan stern, femmay coiner phrezz. Pity you heaven gawchaw tepra cotta. Wooder bin soma cheesier. Ha-wephyr. Zye seng. Ah, here smissis Crone wither teen bikkies. (*Enter: Mrs Crone, muttering. She puts down on the desk a tray sparsely loaded with Earl Grey, Garibaldis and Spode. She sniffs and, wiping her palms on her thighs, exits.*)

Morrison: long story short, this Gloria dame tell Snorm she smatter battim. Seshie carn liver thattim. Weller course Reg, who spinner wye caller time, welly snoggener jar sly there orla time an do narten. Noppeye a long shot. Sewey says, Normie says, Norm, Juno watcher doon? Hacker newpie sarcher dilly says. A Norm turn zonnim, knee says, yicken go an get—

Lauder: Sugar?

Morrison: Ear, swun-lum, please—stuffty says. Anna neck-sing you know thesser tourvem shaper narp toohey charther. Inner meantime Gloria—

Lauder: Prep sugared meckit cleah, in your rotticle, that ay em bay no means wan of those cheps in a knavery tar. Wan hezz wan's feet firmleh on the grond. Fay fermleh. Ave trade (cossit's fewter jodge) but wan hezz trade to wintra juice a certain, wash lair sair, a certain late hottedness, even a certain leviteh. Weir thottercoss seckrificing wan cinter lectual integriteh. And now, hammer Fred, fuel forgive meh—

Morrison: spin darple crossnem. She spin goa gnat with this pubkeeper bloke. Bertsy snime. Reel drongo toohey yizz. Now wee calm zinter the pitcher. He crasher zinter the tent, anny dussy splock, see. An Gloria hassy stirricks. Birchy scream zairt, key-patter this Birchy says. Ony by this timer corsair rawl stinko. Honour turp, shuno. Soshie cesstwim Birchy says—

Lauder: aimer soss cuter—

Morrison: Gedadda this, anatomy sight frevver. So then Bert pick supper nempty bottle anny letser maffit. Clobber zemmorl. Givsem a reel goa nova.

Lauder: excuse meh. Herpule forgive meh, but aim sliffue. Hefter gerta a T-chin a toppers four. (*He goes to the door and calls Mrs Crone, who enters, running.*)

Mrs Crone: Watsy up to?

Morrison: Ear, by this time there's a reel blue on, a niss feller—

Lauder: Fay ness toof sinew again, Morrison. Fay nessin deed. Myrrh stin-sting discussion. Glare toof binner phelp. Wom stollwez tretter beer phelp to wan skolligs. (*With Mrs Crone's help, he prises Morrison from his chair, and together they drag him towards the door.*)

Morrison: Bert snow slouch wennit kumpster— (*Exit.*)

Welph cosshude know best.
Emmince shodge ob.
B'toff trol
A. M. peng frit.
Neddu phil rother
strongleh
thet thet omchair
rother kleshes
wither coppet.
Lesker triddervem birth

Welph core swonken
see your point
meddier chep.
An womsted
mitchoom steffer
fakey knifer colour.
Bar chaw way funo,
shiss fay fondoff thet
omchair,
a nolso the coppet

Swan-upping

You may have read somewhere, as I have, that swan-upping is the practice of marking young swans and cygnets for their owners, and that annual expeditions are made for this purpose on the Thames. A likely story! Who would ever want to own a swan? They are notoriously savage and capricious birds, and capable of breaking your leg with one sweep of their powerful wings. The truth is that there is no such thing as swan-upping. It is just a crazy fantasy dreamed up by a Putney accountant who, from professional habit, couldn't bear to think that there was nothing on the credit side to offset that undeniably debit substance known as swans*down*.

Max Dobbs was tossing restlessly in bed one night in his comfortable home in Putney. Before going to bed he had noticed, on his wife's dressing table, along with the other cosmetic paraphernalia, a large powderpuff in a cut-glass bowl. Remember, this was back in the thirties, when everyone's wife had these things. He picked it up idly and asked his wife what the hell it was. His wife, Letty, explained that it was a swansdown puff. A slight frown appeared momentarily on Max's brow, and he said 'Oh' in a preoccupied way, and that's all there was to it—then. It was only later, when racked by insomnia, that he reopened the subject.

'Essay, Lettair? Is it trooleh colled thet? Emmean, rillian trooleh?'

'Swot col dwot? Mex? Eh do wishooed tretter gerta sleep.'

'Thet poff thing, Lettair? Is it trooleh, emmean *onslair*, called swansdon?'

'Erfa heffen seck, Mex. What's it metter? Gerta sleep, dear. You wirmpy in a fit stet to tocktwol thur smenter morrow few dirnt get some sleep.'

There was a few minutes' silence, during which Letty went back to sleep.

'But if it's trooleh swansdon, Lettair...Lettair! Ewer weck?' As there was no reply he gently jabbed her soft white form with his forefinger—or, rather, what he imagined to be gently, but his finger, after twenty-five years at the adding machine, was like steel, and his wife woke up screaming.

'My God, Mex! What is it?'

'Fraffly sorreh, earl girl. Didn't minter denchew. But, well, demmer tol, Lettair, if it's swansdon, there mospeh a swanop. Dirn chewer gree? Emmean there mospeh. Zol the riz to it.' He switched on the light and lit a cigarette.

'Max, ditchu teck your Hollix? Mex, eddu bleeve youfa gawchaw Hollix.'

Without replying, Max got out of bed and started to get dressed. 'Esspurze,' he said, pulling on a pair of rubber waders, 'the sponter beer swan or two on the riverret now, at this verreh merment. Sorra copple urnleh the smonning. Brecking a yong chep sleg. Gosstleh business, blod everywhere. Sotcher nommer swings.' He took a sou'-wester out from under the pillow and put it on his head.

'Mex, wherrer you girng?'

'Jaw stonter the river, dear.' He took his grandfather's old muzzleloader down from over the mantelshelf, and squinted down the barrel. 'Whesser totch, dear? The wommith a new bettriz? Ah, hee-wee or. Shompy long.'

Left alone, Letty stared for a long time at the vacant space over the mantelshelf. Gradually her eyes closed, and she dropped off to sleep again. About an hour later she was awakened by the sound of a shot. She sat up in bed with her heart pounding. Soon she heard the front door being opened and closed, and a minute later Max entered the room. He was dripping wet and had a scratch on his left cheek.

'Mex, what was that shot?'

'Nothing, dear. No swans. Botter coss wonker noddliex pecktit this temmer the year. Emmean they've probblair teckna mollter Henleh or some goffersecken pless—for the swore-nopping.'

'For the what?'

'The swore-nopping.' He cleared his throat defiantly, and took off his waders. 'Zurnleh seng to Chris the other deh, spot tem they got on with the swore-nopping. You nir, dear, mocking the yong swans for their owners. Cygnets too. Jolleh good idea. Sprezzed so few pipple noah bottit.'

'But what was that shot, Mex?'

'Cong seg seckleh. Somthing domber the river. Thot ed better shoot it.' He climbed back into bed, removed his sou'-wester and put it back under the pillow. He turned out the light and fell into a deep and dreamless sleep—happy at last to have given expression to the repressed creative talents which he had always felt were in him. After all, a man has to be a real poet to invent swan-upping.

Members Only

Com beck, com beck, Law Chemplin, please,
Ang keepar spure ang clean.
Act 1, Scene 2, Line 4. See? *Knees!*
D'skossting air-knob seen.

The verreh thot of nuditeh…
Nway Congo wan. Jar skont!
Sar choffle bistleh cruditeh.
A spadders Cholleh Zont.

Meh dotter's still at school and yet
Ah-neppleh discovers,
In Rirmy Owen Juliet,
'A perref stock-rossed l----s!'

We know these things in midder ledge,
Yet still fill shokka bottom.
Bar chorleh, Sir—not on the stedge!
Nir nid to tokka bottom.

Now, hee-wee hev, Pedge 21,
A reference to 'hip-joint'.
Bar tamer sliffue now and run
To meh feffret Soho strip joint.

The Old Games

It is a great tragedy that so many of the old street games, such as 'Hurting Gertie' and 'Razors Alive-Oh', have disappeared from the London scene, or have changed so much over the years that little of their original zest and excitement remains.

Fortunately, not all these old games have vanished under the corrosive influence of television and bingo. 'Fireman's Bluff', although strictly speaking not a street game, is still played occasionally. All you need is a trainload of passengers on the Underground and a small fire of sufficient intensity to bring the train to a halt between two stations. The idea of the game, which may be played solo, is to see if you can induce a fellow passenger to say something (ten points), to complain of the discomfort (fifty points), or to leave his or her strap and climb out through a window (a hundred points, or bullseye).

The last time I played Fireman's Bluff the conditions were ideal. The train was filled with greenish smoke, and the tunnel outside lit by a red glow. I turned to the man beside me and said, 'Look sleck we meppy incinerated.' His reply was, 'Hmm.' He didn't actually open his mouth, but I gave myself ten points just the same.

Another amusing game, played in bus queues, is 'Softening Up Nannie'. As an almost full bus approaches, you lunge heavily at the old woman in front of you, thus beating her to the only available seat. As the bus moves off without her, you call out, 'Fraffly sorreh.' Your opponent laughs happily, and calls back, 'Honour to tol. Fiffly caned a fume shore.' There is no scoring in this game; your reward is the deep satisfaction that comes from having made a friend, and from knowing that the spirit of the playing fields of Eton is with us still.

But perhaps the most interesting of all these pastimes is 'Baiting the Chum', or 'Sting'. Only two can play, and the idea is to see who can make the other lose his, or her, temper first, using no equipment other than a nimble wit and a flexible tongue. It goes something like this:

'Bobra, dolling. Thottit mospeh you. Reckeg nezz choc-koat. Eh *volk*wez admired that coat.'

'Oh, it's you, Wilma! Eh thot for a merment it was—ah, how *is* your mother, dear?'

'Mommeh zoffter spennerken a shooshol. Hoz Ronald? *Dear* Ronald. Still as chomming a zephyr—isn't he?'

'Sedger since wif sinew, Wilma dolling. We thotchew *mettef* binnet the Empseh the other night. Butter coshew weren't. Esspurze you most live sotch a full life there at—ah, Meddeh Vel.'

'Becker Strit, dolling, ectuelleh. Nir, fotchnettleh, stern dot, we were rah-nebble to be there. Cholz was fraffly busier shooshol. You nirhow they ol lean on him. Put Cholz, sotch a gret responsibiliteh. Coss bing so *yong* mexa difference.'

'Dit Cholz. Is he still—ah, does he still—emmean, ah, how *is* Sophie, bether weh? Heaven sinner fredges. Bar twocker dwonnex pecked? Emmean, well, you noah temmean.'

'*Dear* Sophie. Sotch a dear frender fozz. Her new hosband's chomming.'

'You know, Wilma, somtems I do *envy* you. Emmean the *simple* life you mar sleed. How *lockeh* you are, rilleh. Excuse me dear, a little dendruff on your collar. Emmean, to be sort of *innocent*. Moffless rilleh—chaw redge.'

'Oh, hee-wee or at Clerridges. Emma sliffue, dolling. Shell wishy be sing you on Chew-stair? Nir, nir coshew wirmpy *there*. Bye, Bobra dolling. Youshered go hirm, dolling. Youlk tired. Bye, dolling. Law-fleff toof sinew.'

'Bye, Wilma dolling. Oh, Wilma, bether weh—there's something you wotter nir. Sarah and I were wondering a fwishered tell you…oh, hizzer texi. Bye, dolling.'

Sway thing,
Kleddies n Gentlemen,
the chew-lolla gree
with mih whennay seh,
femmay coiner phrezz,
we raw linner grimment.

A nah wesher losk
Leddie Mogret to,
hosh lair sair, to
sephew words

Omster Chemmen,
lairtsin gentlemen,
thairk yoch.

War nizzen deed trooleh
quare turver whelmed.

Netch relleh wong con
tollwez biquette shore
the twonner zon the
rate poth.

Bar twommer stollwez
tretter bishaw.

Frog zomple…

An interesting and vigorous game between skilled and evenly matched performers. W's opening gambit is reminiscent of the Feuerbach-Wolanski system, but the counter-attack which B assembles is indeed a solid one, and W quickly loses the initial advantage. Towards the end of the middle game B shows signs of sudden collapse, but the introduction of 'innocent' is a brilliant move, worthy of Kludopkin or Fiorelli. Finally, the arrival of the taxi enables B to have that most valuable last word. Yes, altogether a most interesting match.

Three Cheers

Britannia wants roold the wevs,
Bot noshie wevs the rules.
A swellers kings we noffaned nevs
In nollar poblic schools.

Britannia, this lenderphope
Ung glorry fosso long,
Ears nowprie ocku ped with dope,
En dwimmin, wanen song.

Og lorrier Sempah is no more;
Instead—a Commonwealth,
Weck commonwealthy pipple pour
Osskotch to drink their health.

Bar twirse! In mocket plessen square,
Ong common nendon green,
It's Common Mocket evreh where;
On evreh telleh screen.

Emmedgen hoppor Deddeh would
Hev fotta kenstar rentreh;
Hop roddy was; eng gleddy could
Mick sirnleh with the gentreh.

Moon Man Go Home!

To a visitor, the great fascination of London lies in the many little-known places of interest that are tucked away where one would never expect to find them, so that even many Londoners do not know of their existence. Perhaps the most interesting of all is the recently opened Tempotron, conveniently situated at Hyde Park Corner. This is the only place in London where one may travel into the future.

The procedure is simple. A uniformed attendant shows you to your capsule. You settle into a comfortable seat, fasten your seat belt and shut the door. You set the controls in front of you to the date and time of day to which you want to travel. Then you press a button, and off you go—into the future.

Don't be alarmed by the faint nausea you will feel; this disappears in a minute or two, and the shuddering motion is not unpleasant once you get used to it. And in any case, you won't be there long, as each decade only takes a few seconds to pass. You are advised not to travel too far into the future, as no guarantee can be given that the Tempotron will still be there when you arrive at your destination.

My last journey, made about a week ago, was to the year 2050. It was most enjoyable, and well worth the few shillings it cost. I found London much the same as it is today, except for one or two minor changes, the most noticeable being that the whole of Hyde Park had been converted into a supermarket. Here I was able to buy, for a few britcents, three of my books which I haven't yet written.

A large block of workers' flats extended along the northern side of Piccadilly from Park Lane to the big monorail station and rocket-launching complex at what is now Green Park Underground. Most of the people I saw were wearing tracksuits of some glossy synthetic material, with embroidered badges on their backs carrying such slogans as

Let Smair Kloff, Emma Seck Smenniac and *Fraffly Well Spoken*. But apart from these details the general scene was very much as it is today, and I saw quite a few rolled umbrellas and translucent plastic bowlers.

I called in at the President's Arms, a pub on the corner of Quant Street and Lennon Lane, and ordered a zozz and soda. I sat down at a corner table and struck up a conversation with my neighbour, a rather prosperous-looking young chap of about thirty. His tracksuit was a brilliant magenta, matching the colour of his beard, which was worn long, and plaited into a sort of under-chin pigtail and tied with a bow of old school ribbon. I asked him how long the President's Arms had been there, explaining that I had only just returned to London after a long absence.

'Cont seg seckleh,' he replied. 'Emps prezzed you dirnt remembrit though. Spinnier slong a zecken remembah.'

'Chomming little pless,' I said. We chatted about this and that for a while, then he said, 'Drink a top earl chep,' and asked me if I'd like another. As he was at the bar ordering the drinks, I noticed that the slogan on his back was *Moon Man Gir Hirm!*

When he came back I asked him if he was a Londoner. He looked mildly dismayed. 'Netch-relleh, earl chep. Whey chew osk? Herpay dirnt looklegger foreigner. Thol jura spectre coss. Whetchew kom from, bether weh? Comm pless your recksent.'

I told him Australia, and asked if he had ever been there.

'Well, earce, ectuelleh. Thether smonning ay think. Smeshing little pless.'

As I was intrigued by his Moon Man badge, and having seen other references to Moon Men on my previous visit, about forty years later, in 2090, I contrived in an oblique way, to introduce the subject.

'Ah, these Moon Men,' I said, shaking my head and sighing. 'Nosteh business.'

'Earce, earce, gosstleh. Airpsleh gosstleh. Wong conner medgin hir we leffer gair tridder the little cheps. Ol the President's falter coss.

Demmertol Mogret,
chep zirnia winker monda.
Snort ziffy was
an F. I. Smoshel.
Feller rotterby
cot moshelled.
Gairdwee do things
bettrin the yommy.
Arrer member beckon 47,
or meffpin 48.
Any wet was in Tripoli.
No, meffpin
Nelleck-zendri-yaw

Earce. Ears of coss.
End now, meddier Colonel,
Prep shoot lacquer
little something tweet.
Eddu wishooed trair
little tickteck.
A nah wemma sliffue.
Wim steffer nother
little toxoon.
A nah waim skir

Theshered nair freff binnin vated in the fur spless. Plesser swomming withem.'

I commiserated with him, and said we had had a lot of trouble with them in Australia too, but that the situation was gradually being brought under control. I hoped he wouldn't ask me how.

'Trob liz,' he said, 'wonker never be shore of binger low nenny maw. Little cheppser so demmed invisible. Joster bitter lock they're so smol and relatively hommless.'

At this stage I happened to look down and noticed that the laces of my left shoe had been tied into a knot with those of my right. Then to my amazement I felt something tugging at my left ear. I twisted around sharply, but there was no one in sight. It was an unnerving experience.

'Trob liz,' my companion was saying, 'wong compy shore what scone tweppen next—aaaaagh!' He shouted out suddenly; some invisible creature had pulled his pigtail beard violently.

'Lesker dotter this, earl chep,' we both said simultaneously. We walked quickly outside, leaving our drinks unfinished.'

'Weh lemmer sliffue,' said my companion, going over to his minicopter at the parking meter. 'Hefter girt Welleska softernoon.'

As I walked back to the Tempotron I wondered vaguely whether there was anything I could do to prevent the arrival on the planet of these irritating little creatures. But here it was, 2050, and they were already here. Obviously, I had left it too late.

Yeppet yousha nut.
Ifer gotta natter
speak Fraffly.
Ipey nwirkin
forpa fesser Lauder,
a nair wiker nony
talk Strine.
It kinder getcher,
few Noah timene.
Fried eye car nelpew

Well, dibboy, wimce
trair little hodder.
A noshol we tray
wan smore?
Reddeh? Repee tofter me:
The wren in Spen
is mennleh in the
pline.
Ir, fraffly sorreh,
Emmean the wren
is in the plen

Brain Drain

Ontil the edge of thirty-nine
Ed nevah heard of dollars.
Wan toed the youshol Cembridge line
With gentlemen and scholars.

A spora smace within a church,
We lived in digser netticks.
We revel din ah piora search
And heyer methemetics.

Wan smenken surn was Britain's fem;
And Britain's commerce flourished.
And, spottsmer nol, wip led the kem,
Though slettleh undernourished.

Bes-skinning flints, en perring cheese,
Wim-mennedge donna few pence.
But now—the yicker nommic freeze!
And salaries in new pence!

Ev don meh bit for Britain's gairn.
Although both bredden born here,
The dren is mennleh of the bren—
Eh moffta California.

I Cannot Tell a Lie

Just why did George Washington chop down that cherry tree? Now, I have no wish to precipitate an international crisis by disturbing the delicate balance of that 'special relationship' between Britain and the United States. Washington is one of America's special heroes, and the story about how he could not tell a lie after having chopped down a cherry tree is one of the key pieces in the jigsaw puzzle of American folklore. But facts are facts, and recently discovered evidence seems to prove conclusively that the popular version of the incident is not entirely accurate.

To begin with, it wasn't George Washington; it was Isaac Newton. And it wasn't a cherry tree; it was an apple tree. Finally, it wasn't an ordinary axe; it was a rather primitive electric hatchet which the young Newton had just invented. He had been experimenting with electricity, and by flying a kite up into the storm clouds had succeeded in drawing off a steady flow of about twelve volts—just enough to drive his hatchet. Naturally, he wanted to see all his energy and ingenuity put to use immediately. Not wanting to tramp through his mother's house in muddy booties (he was only two years old at the time), he abandoned the idea of removing a leg from the kitchen table, and set to work on a nearby apple tree. In a few minutes the mighty monarch of the orchard was teetering. 'Timber!' shouted the infant Isaac, and down it came—apples and all.

Young Newton, standing among the fallen apples, could see the gravity of the situation, and started to run for cover. But it was too late. His mother, hearing the commotion, came running from the house. 'Isaac!' she called. 'What gostleh contrevence a few binnin venting now? Rilleh, dibboy, har tosser mew are.' Isaac, being too little and too late, was nonplussed—but not for long.

'Bedge Irve, mater,' he said. 'Jolleh close, earl kel. Dem think strock beh lettning. Nosteh business. Essay, mater, jaw slooket ol those epples. Ed better go to my den and stot inventing cider.' He started to toddle towards the house, but unfortunately tripped over the flex and fell into the mud, still clutching the hatchet. From then on the conversation went something like this:

'Hir many tems,' his mother said, 'a few bin turled: dirnt lie!'

'$x^2+20x+z$,' came back the quick reply. He had a little dog with him, no bigger than a logarithm. 'Come, Napier,' said the little tot, and called him to his knee. '14+9 is quite a lot. It zolmurst 23. Now, do not let this trouble you, but $4^2=w$.'

'You niddent think,' his mother said, 'you'll get away with that! Jaw slooker-doll the mare-shoove med, you nawteh little brat.' And off she went to get the strap, to castigate the little chap. The prodigy, now left alone, reflected on his fate. He chawed at little Napier's bone, and multiplied by 8. And, as he was at loss for words, by $x+7\ 2/3$.

'It sklitter meh,' he said at last, with infinite regret. 'The present cannot be the past. The future swither syet.' A beating! Nothing could be worse in his expanding universe. 'Oh, mater dear, do beer brick'—he didn't flinch or run—'dirnt layer tonn *too* jolleh thick. xy+4+1.' He put aside his famous hatchet, and prayed to Peter, Pawl and Ratchet.

On this historical occasion, you'll be relieved to hear, the mass and energy equation was not at all severe. Little Isaac took his beating, then invented central heating. 'Wan thenks wan slocky stozz,' he cried, and raised his eyes to heaven, then trotted happily inside, dividing by 11. He asked, 'War chell-we hev for tea? Once choster scovered grevity.'

One Lump or Two?

Woo-choo keffra nother cup, dear?
China blend, of coss, from Twinings;
Little pecks with silver linings.
Come now, dolling, drink it up, dear.

Krimmin chooker? Don't refuse
A sennwich. Hem? No, thet's cucumbah.
Heffue sin the letter snumbah
Of the *Illustretted News*?

On yolleft knee pootchaw plett, dear;
On your rett, chock-uppen sossa.
(Prep swan shouldn't tretta fossa;
Off terol, she sirnleh ett, dear.)

Ah, what poise, what flair, what dash!
Chomming menners, and sir sweet.
Prep shooed lecksum mottu eat?
My God! My Royal Worcester! Crash!

The Changing Guards

Many visitors to London have asked why the Guards at Bucking-ham Palace never speak when on duty, and why they stamp their feet so much and so noisily. In the old days things were so different. It was the usual thing for the Guards to talk to whoever happened to be around. They answered questions freely about such things as life in the Palace, troop movements, and the location of public conveniences. They sold souvenirs, joined in impromptu picnics, and allowed themselves to be photographed in warlike poses with family groups from Minnesota and Rhode Island; and the only time they stamped their feet was when attacked at ground level by venomous spiders, or when plagued by some private frustration.

However, like so many other good things in Britain, all this had to come to an end. It was an unfortunate incident in 1954 that finally made the authorities decide to enforce the more standoffish attitude that now prevails.

It was a warm sunny afternoon, and Guard No. 40-7X/399, Reg Poulteney, a native of Wyong in New South Wales, was relaxing with his chums near the main Palace gates. In those days anyone was admitted to the Guards—even Australians, there being no discrimination on grounds of nationality, race, creed, colour or language. Young Reg and his mates were playing darts with a couple of retired steel men from Pittsburgh. As it was against the regulations to fasten a dartboard to the Palace gates or railings, they had, as usual, hired an Indian student, Choobli Dar, to act as dartboard holder-upper: a duty he undertook willingly as he was paid twopence an hour for his services. This was a lot of money to one who had subsisted for most of his life on a daily handful of cardamom seeds and the smell of a ghee-rag. It enabled

The long tir
mimper-keshens
ock-wetter lomming.

Wan zurnli tweck zemmin
the fex tree-laze
thet a smol group
of fay lodge compnez
will fay shottleh domnet
the industreh.

Ennay thing came rate
in seng thappaphore long
the nombrof tare-curvers
shling cree skrettleh

Earce, Grairgref costier.

Look, Grairgrair,
Omshore that Swilma
in thet fiffle gomment.

Womsted mitchy look
sex trimmleh odd.

Thench yollware stid.

Ah, Wilma dear,
How trooleh chomming
you look.

Dossen chee, Grairgrair?

him to continue his studies, and still left him enough for the iodine he needed for the occasional puncture in the thorax from a carelessly aimed dart.

'Nother beer?' asked Reg, moving over to the empty Oxo carton which served them as a table, and opening up a bottle of brown ale. 'Water bat chews?' he asked, turning to the Americans. 'Ed? Alvin? User lavva nother, woanchez?' He poured the beer out into paper cups and handed them around to the steel men and to his fellow Guards, Quincy Marlborough and Andrew (Buggsy) Molyneux. Then, with a typical gesture of Australian hospitality, he tore off a corner of the Oxo carton, dipped it into his own cup of beer, which held more than the others, and rammed the saturated cardboard into the Indian's mouth. 'Have a suck, mate,' he said, grinning in a friendly manner so that his gold incisors gleamed in the warm July sunlight.

'Goo chur,' said Quincy. 'Womsken grettcher lettcher. What a moffler skrosp of the ot of brewing. Airpsleh moffler spear.' He took another mouthful and savoured its rich brown coal-tar goodness.

'Smeshing,' said Buggsy. 'Womsted mittit texnor Strellian to mecca good hirm-brew. Tess leck trickle. Smeshing.' He wiped the sweet sepia froth from his moustache.

'Mighty fine beer,' said Alvin, 'but where I calm from, back in Pittsburgh…'

'Mighty fine beer,' said Ed, 'but where I calm from, back in Pittsburgh…' He was interrupted by a violent fit of coughing from the Indian student, who had accidentally swallowed the cardboard.

'Knock it orf, mate,' said Reg to the Indian, giving him a friendly kick. 'Yicken put dan that dartboard now, few wanna, an knock orfra smoko.'

They all sat down in the sun, with their backs against the railings, and discussed the various topics of the day—women, the price of beer and the current economic squeeze. Reg, whose feet gave him a lot of trouble, took off his heavy boots and stretched his toes. The Indian took a small paper bag from the folds of his turban, helped himself to a cardamom seed, and sniffed vigorously at his ghee-rag.

'Funny thing hairpner me a carpler yizzer go, wen I was sleeper-cutting dannier Cooma...' But whatever it was that happened will never be known. He jumped to his feet with an angry shout. 'Look!' He screeched. 'That lousy little drongo's tiken me boots!' In the distance they could see Choobli Dar running towards Admiralty Arch, the dartboard clutched in one hand and Reg Poulteney's, or rather Her Majesty's, boots in the other. In spite of the enormous weight he was carrying he made good progress, and very soon vanished from sight.

'Foreign cad,' said Quincy. 'Nidser good whore swipping. Titchmer lesson.'

'Boundah!' said Buggsy, getting to his feet and helping himself to a quick beer while the others were not looking. Then, suddenly, he shouted, '*Cave Regina*, cheps! Here's the boss.' He jumped to attention and saluted, unfortunately forgetting that his right hand still held a cup of beer.

'Crikey!' cried Quincy, scrambling to his feet and saluting.

'Stoner crows!' said Reg. In a desperate effort to avoid being seen without his boots he tried to hide in the Oxo carton, but in his hurry he tripped over a steel man, and fell headlong—just as the royal car arrived at the gates.

The Americans exchanged glances. 'Let sketterhell art a this,' said Ed.

'Looks bad for Uncle Sam,' said Alvin. They collected their cameras and their pictures of their wives and children, and moved away.

'Guess they'll be drummed out of the regiment,' said Ed. 'Whatever that means.'

'Guess so,' said Alvin.

And so, as a result of this incident, still another little bit of Merrie England vanished into the past. Up till then everyone had taken for granted all the fun and souvenir selling, the lighthearted conversation, the picnics and the photography; these seemed both normal and reasonable. But for a Guardsman to be seen without his boots! Well, really, the line had to be drawn somewhere.

There was no fuss, of course; the whole thing was handled with great discretion. But soon, about eight years later, a directive was issued forbidding any more fraternisation. And feet, from now on, were to be stamped at regular intervals, so that no Guard may ever forget, when on duty, that he is wearing boots.

Tea Please

Homenny bins, I yosked, *meck fev?*
Not knowing what I quett-ment.
Bot three, he said. His fesswer skrev
With British onder-stettment.

A fewer chodged with theft or frod,
I yosked, *What compromise*
Woo chewer dopt? He loft, *Good Lord,*
It zoller pecker flies.

Seh yorron fire, or prepshaw dead,
I yosked, *War twoochoo do?*
A British gentleman, he said,
Will lollweh smoddle through.

Agreat deal has been written about the British genius for under-statement, for compromise, and for muddling through. Why is it then that we hear so little about 'restaurant coffee', which is surely the ultimate embodiment of these peculiarly British qualities? Under-statement, because it is called 'coffee'—a very mild description indeed. Compromise, because it often tastes like tea. And if it were not for a perfect example of muddling through, this strange stimulant would never have seeped through to the eating houses of London.

I had called to see my old friend Osbert Porbeagle, a well-known tea merchant and importer. When I entered the room I was overwhelmed by an odd and unpleasant smell. It was a combination of smells;

pungent yet flat, acrid yet dull. It brought back memories of mice and old caves. It reminded me vaguely of quinic acid (one of the tetra-hydroxy-cyclohexane-carboxylic group) which, as everyone knows, is obtained from, among other things, cinchona bark and coffee beans. Neither Osbert nor his pallid secretary, to whom he was dictating a letter, seemed be disturbed by this odd smell.

'H'lo earl chep,' he said, in answer to my coughing, 'shompier merment. Ah, um, Miss Flench, ah, yes. It hair snoppean therefore deemed precticable, in view of theer foss-ed termnetion of contrectual orplikeshens bitwin your goodself and the ondersigned, toopra seed with the distribution of the relevant emolumentation prior to dehumidifying the fotty kesses of brirken orange pekoe referred toon yollettah of the fotteen thinst. Yoss fethfulleh.'

I could see, on a small table, a saucepan boiling briskly over a spirit stove. The air was thick with fumes. I asked Osbert what was cooking.

'Freddeh con tellier. Tret sickret,' he replied. 'Bar tweeber leevit has grecker mershol paw spillties. A gnaw Tony thet, wonken be pretty shaw itlin dew smore pipple to drink tea.'

'But what is it?' I asked again. 'It smells like one of the tetra-hydroxy-cyclohexane-carboxylic group.'

'Beg edger rate,' he said. 'Nother word, scoffee. Foreign beverage. Youmair furdavit.'

Having recently tasted coffee in Italy and in America, I found this statement hard to believe. I pressed him for more details, and the whole sordid story came out. Years previously he had bought up a job lot of jetsam, thinking that it consisted of esparto grass, for his tea business. When the bales were opened they were found to contain only small brown beans. One of his foremen, an Italian, identified them as coffee, so they were stored away in a remote warehouse and forgotten, until recently, some ten years later. Age had not improved them; they were badly charred by fire, and impregnated by the camphor and creosote with which they had been stored. However, not liking to see them go

On the burning deck of the Hesperus
The Yenchent Merriner stood.
Endy credder lod: 'Nir trespassers!
Gir beckter Birnham Wood!'

Andy crade to the weird sisters,
'Youm sko wither breckof dawn.'
End the hot deck gair fim blisters
Bessade the yellion corn.

'Plair yoppen plether kem,' he cursed,
'Meckingdom forra sword!
Nah hooshel bither firstu burst
Into the goddon, Maude?'

to waste, Osbert had tried a few experiments, hoping that a marketable product would emerge. It was the final one of these experiments that I was now watching.

'Gad, I think the smeppy yit!' he said, when he had recovered from the choking fit that had overtaken him when he removed the lid from the saucepan. He held a handkerchief over his face, and peered into the mess. 'Simpler nofftu. We burned it a little more, to bring ot the flevver, you know. Grondit op fane. Edded a little solfah, to give it body. Boiled it for a few dez. A nee-wee orra tlost, coffee!' He poured some into a cup, and called to his secretary.

'Ah, Miss Flench, ed lecku to trair little coffee.'

'A little what, Mr Porbeagle?' She looked horrified. 'Eh thot this was the fertlezzer.'

'Nir, nir, coffee. A new foreign drink. Greppor spillties.'

'New! *Foreign!* Oh, no, *please*, Mr Porbeagle.'

'Come, come, Miss Flench,' he insisted, handing her the evil-looking brew. 'Wan lomp or two? Cosser trilleh nidser slesser lemon.'

Miss Flench took a small sip. Then another. Finally she drank it all, with apparent relish. 'Or you shore it's foreign, Mr Porbeagle?' she said. 'It squett nace. Tesslake mod, delicious.'

He poured her another cup, and one for himself. 'There sirnleh a smolper centage of modnit,' he said. 'Dew think quishered edda treffle more? Em thinking mennleh of the rare straw tread.'

He added a little more mud from a jar labelled 'Best quality Thames upper reaches', and boiled it up again. Finally they were both satisfied that it was the perfect after-dinner drink; after dinner, that is, of *Faggot Bolognese* and *Rhubarb Flan Béchamel*.

May Mem Was

Though General Muffler; now in chodge,
Simmed slettleh in a dezz,
The sitcher weshen, by n'lodge,
Was comm—to coin a phrezz.

The Pettriots, wan mossted mit,
Ken sturver whelming odds,
Were decent; we were rareleh hit
By foreign feyring squads.

Unrooleh mobs of rioters
(A pritteh kettler fish)
From tem to tem would cry at us:
'Ah-lo nose-picking Glish!'

Ompleasant olterkeshens hed
Epperentleh occurred;
A coppalov are cheps went med,
And letter on, a third.

Sir Phillip (now Lord) Vernal, who
Had rissentleh returned,
Was chatting with the Colonel, who
Was rother bedleh burned.

Sir Andrew (now Lord) Kletterer
I hadn't met before.
Etc. etc.
For seven volumes more.

The Strange Case of Scottle and Jodd

'Ready, Jim?' said Samuel Johnson, looking up from his manuscript. 'Well, as I was saying—Quote, Sir, when a man is tired of London comma he is tired of life. End of quote.'

Now, this statement has the ring of truth, but, as with so many similar statements—such as *In vino veritas*, and *Homo sapiens*—the ring is not so much of truth as of plausibility. There are, in fact, quite a number of men who are tired of London, and yet not tired of life—and Scottle and Jodd are two of them. So would anyone be tired of London if they had that job; either cooped up all day in those dingy rooms or flying about in high-powered cars to the scene of one ridiculous and usually justifiable homicide after another. What happens in some ghastly provincial village when Sir Giles is found face downwards on the floor with his head missing? The Chief Constable takes his pipe out of his mouth, raises his shaggy eyebrows, and says, 'Fred Weems Colin Scottle and Jodd.'

We visited Scottle and Jodd recently, and asked them what they thought about all this, and whether they are, or are not tired of life. They both said that they are indeed heartily sick of London, and of being at the beck and call of half-witted local constabularies in remote villages where you can't even get a decent meal. They are sick of all the pipe-smoking and tea-drinking they are subjected to in these places, and in which they are expected to join. Scottle suffers from mild but chronic tannin poisoning from the tea, and Jodd is allergic to tobacco and comes out in blotches whenever anyone lights up, but they are by no means tired of life. Scottle's ambition is to get out of the racket as soon as possible and devote his time and energy to making model ships out of used matches; and he wants to live in Paris. Jodd can hardly wait for his retirement, so that he can open a strip joint in Majorca. 'Then you would say, gentlemen,' I asked them, 'that you are not tired of life?'

'Bare Jerve and/or Gad, sir. No!' said Detective Superintendent Scottle. He took his pipe from his pocket, and took a couple of bubbly drags at it. Sergeant Jodd sneezed noisily. 'Listen, Guvner, you prommer smee. Noppaphore lunch.' He looked aggrieved. He turned to me and said, 'Blimey, guv, I'm not sick of life. Cor matey coo bless your heart, guv, I'm just sick of falling through trapdoors in Limehouse. Lookered me. Sopping!' He squelched his boots, and sneezed again. 'Gorblimey luvaduck coo guvner toff cor. It's all very well and not arfbad for 'im.' He jerked his head resentfully towards his colleague. 'E. gets all the limelight; all I get's Limehouse. Heh heh heh. Eh, guv?' He leered at me unpleasantly, waiting for me to laugh. Obviously he had made his quip many times. Scottle raised his eyes to the ceiling, and sighed with the tedium of it all, and muttered, 'Aw, shut up, you little punk.'

'But surely, gentlemen,' I said, 'You must derive great satisfaction from the fact that you belong to such a…(here I was forced to consult my notes) such a fine body of men? I mean the *esprit de corps* and all that?'

The two men exchanged a brief and mutually hostile glance. 'Fine body, nuts!' said Scottle. 'Air spreamy foot,' said Jodd.

The telephone rang. 'Don't answer it, guv,' said Jodd. 'Please. Wait till me feet are dry, guv.'

'Look, earl chep,' said Scottle, getting up from his desk and beckoning to me. He went over to the constable sitting at a nearby desk, and gave him a gentle push. The constable fell to the floor and remained there motionless. He then went over to another constable who was standing in an alcove, holding two cups of tea, and prodded him on the nose. The constable rocked gently backwards and forwards, but never blinked. 'See?' said the Detective Superintendent. 'Theshaw fane boddier men, sir. Dummies! Oldjer sploddeh dummies! Ol the government's falter coss. The yick-nomic freeze. Gad, sir. Do you wonder em sicker Flondon?' He laughed bitterly. 'Jost the tua voss running the hurl shir. Me and thet blotchy little creep.'

Stunned, I asked him how they could possibly handle everything themselves.

'Computers, earl chep, computers. Simpler zeppy sea. Wondjers feeds in the fex on ponched cods. Press a botton, a not coms the murdrer snem. Simpler noff, but josso bloodeh boring. En bing stock with this slob dozen mecca tenny yizzier.' He looked sourly at his wet colleague.

'Beh the weh,' he went on, 'her pewker nonderstend war twifpin tockner bot, but we have to carry on in this ridiculous fashion.' I found him easier to understand now that he was starting to speak English.

'You know, instructions from above,' he continued. 'The export drive and all that.'

Export drive! I was even more stunned. The whole business seemed so improbable. This enormous building of brick and stone, the famous Scotland Yard, with only these two men in it, and hundreds of dummy policemen. And the computers. And now—the export drive! Jodd sniggered at my astonishment. He took off his coat and started to wring the water out of it into a chipped enamel basin on his desk.

'Yes, Mr Um, ah,' said Scottle. 'The fact is that Britain has a large overseas trade in crime paperbacks. In 1967, the last year for which I have the figures, exports of British books totalled something like £46 million. Western Europe alone amounted to about £9 million. Not all paperbacks, of course. Hardback jobs too; non-fiction and so on. But in every country, crime fiction—that's us—is high on the list of favourites.' He took out his pipe again, and lit it. Jodd, who had finished wringing out his coat, and was now idly kicking the stomach of the dummy policeman on the floor, sneezed, and said, 'Aw listen, Jack, it's only ah-pa sleffen. You prommer smee.' But Scottle ignored him.

'Now, our readers,' he said, puffing vigorously at his pipe, 'our readers expect, puff, a certain, puff, long-established ritual from us. And, well, frankly, Mr Um, we've got instructions, puff, and we can't

Ir, Uncle
hock necken vinshue?
Sholleh you con
trillian trooleh
thing cade do thet!
Thee skaned peeplar
urli treng to herlpew.
Omshore
youlpie mar cheppier
with your rir
netch group

Listen to mih, Mebble.
Em steng here.
A nirpty skirnter
meckmy chench memmaned.
A nasher loskew
to remembah the tame
quett kebbeble
of gaying in todge
with messerlisstah.
End nah, plizz,
another brendeh.
This hesser bitter test

let them down. But I won't have to stick it out much longer. Do you happen to have any used matches on you?'

Jodd stared glumly at his sodden boots, and muttered, 'Jeez, you can get sick of falling into canals.' He went over to the window, opened it, and threw out the water from the basin, and watched to see where it landed. 'Nearly got him that time, Jack,' he said as he returned.

By now the telephone was ringing incessantly. 'Shompier merment, earl chep,' said Scottle, resuming his professional voice and manner. 'Better ronce writ.' He braced himself for an instant, then picked up the telephone. 'Scottle and Jodd. G'monning.' There was a long silence while he listened.

'Earce, earce, of cossole chep. Earce, netchrelleh. Wibbie gleddu. Hommneh torsos? Oh, corkscrew, eh? Sond sleckerninsade job. Motch blod? Nir, nir, coss not. We shompy long. Bay earl chep.' He put down the telephone with a sigh. 'Helmsley, Yorkshire. Torsos again. Ah, well,' he said.

Jodd got wearily into his overcoat, and jammed his wet hat onto his head. He looked tired, and blotchier than ever. 'Moats, I suppose,' he said. 'No canals, but moats this time.'

'Oh shut up, Clive,' said Scottle.

Set in a Cupro-nickel Sea

Britannia, a swan seppaphore,
Wants roold the wevs from shore to shore;
Mo spahful, yes, but what is more,
By commerce on the heels of war,
She roold the lands of menneh.

Since Rawleh, Drecken Gookween Bess,
In jongle, veldt and wilderness,
Britannia's word was law—no less;
En devreh colony said: Yes.
But noshie hezzen tenneh.

Todeh, withdron from foreign field;
Withol her skozz of bettle healed;
Withot her trident or her shield;
She is at loskom pelled to yield
Her plesser pon the penneh.

Dog Days

Anyone who will take the trouble to disguise himself as a dog and walk down Knightsbridge on all fours will be rewarded by the completely new vistas which will open up to him, and by the many new friendships which will undoubtedly come his way. However, it is important to remember that the tail should be wagged almost continually, and biting and snarling should be avoided. Even quivering can land you in difficulties. Finally, you should be accompanied by an upright companion on the end of a lead.

Many people in the past have never walked down Knightsbridge in this fashion, and English literature and letters are the poorer for it. Carlyle, for instance, never engaged in this pastime. In fact it is doubtful if he even disguised himself as a dog. The same appears to be true of Ruskin, Dickens, Henry James and the Prince Consort, yet all of them surely, at one time or another, must have passed this way. What can it have been that deterred them? Was it just that they never thought of it?

This can hardly be the explanation; Carlyle and the Prince Consort, must, between them, have thought of everything. No, the only explanation seems to be that they were all too feline in appearance, or that they couldn't wag their tails. But let us put on our dogskins and take a stroll down this famous thoroughfare.

As soon as we get down on all fours we become aware of a subtle and exciting change. Everything seems to take on a new significance; our awareness is heightened and our senses are sharpened. The first thing we notice is that the pavement is extraordinarily hard. The next thing that captures our attention is the infinite and magical variety of the human foot. Finally comes the most exciting discovery of all— we meet, on equal terms, our first dog, and we learn to our amazement that London dogs not only look like their owners, but they also talk like them.

Most of the dogs one meets on these jaunts are extremely friendly. Not long ago I struck up an acquaintance with a most charming Labrador. He was accompanied by a young chap on snowshoes, and wearing a fur cap with earflaps. He came up and addressed me in what I assume to have been his native idiom.

'Howdy, stranger?' he said, 'Mighty fine weather. Mush!' He went over to the gutter and slurped up a mouthful of snow. He complimented me on my winter coat, and sniffed at the zip-fastener with interest. We discussed various topics of mutual interest, such as dog biscuits, cod liver oil and the old 'lamp-post versus tree' controversy. Then suddenly, without even asking where my people came from, he invited me to drop in on him any time and have a bite of pemmican.

I remember also a most interesting conversation I once had with a young black poodle. We happened to be walking in the same direction, and as we came side by side he turned to me and said, 'Dolling, where ditchu get that gosstleh collar?'

'What's wrong with it?' I asked, remembering not to quiver, and falling into step beside him.

'Well, rilleh, dolling. Dirnchew think it's urverdoing it a treffle? Emmean, those feck dammonds. Emmean, ay *osk* you! Kennewer medgin Larry Olivier's dog werren a collar lake thet?'

'I don't like to look too conspicuous,' I said, drawing his attention to the other Knightsbridge dogs.

He looked scornfully at them. 'Noffry sottle,' he said. 'Emmean, off trol, ashered of thot a dog leck you shooder bin more sottle. You nir, plen leather. Coff, preps, or silskin. Prepslittle seddle-stitching. Notso wosten teshess.' He paused, then added, 'Herpew dirnt maned may seng this chaw.'

'Not at all,' I said. 'Very kind of you.'

'Hoddew leck *may* collar?' He lifted up his head so that I could see it properly. It was indeed a very smart collar; plain black calf with a small silver monogram of the letters P. H.

I asked him what they stood for.

'Prince Henrair,' he told me. 'Cossem naw trilleh a prince, you onderstend. That was his idea.' His yellow eyes flickered upwards towards his companion. 'Thoa coss,' he went on, 'wan does hev a rothrim pressive pedigree. '

We walked along in silence for a while, then he turned to me again. 'What shonnem?' he asked. His manner was most direct and friendly.

'Actually, it's—ah, Butch,' I said. 'You know what people are.'

He stopped in his tracks and looked at me in astonishment. 'G'dlord! Thotchu werrer fimmel. Something abot the weh you wokku nir. Fraffly sorreh.' We stopped outside a large hotel. 'Well, Fred Emma sliffue here,' said Prince Henry. 'Swerray live. Ness toove mare-chew—Butch.'

Tempus Fugit

Conservative, dislecking chenge,
With ing-com in the oppah renge,
Meh views meh seem a treffle strenge;
Meh pot a treffle crackish.

The tamer skom to collar halt!
Though Slebber cheps. Itzol their fault.
We Britons, once on earth the salt,
Are nobbot milleh brackish.

En sober said meh bed eh kneel,
Empray: 'Dillod, You should, effeel,
Epplay Yosh-older to the wheel,
And turn it slettleh backish.'

The Widdershins Society was founded in London in 1968 by a group of semi-retired businessmen. Its only aim and object was to promote, as the standard means of recording time in Britain, the 'counter clock', i.e. a clock with the hands moving in the opposite direction to those of all clocks now in use in this country. Those who sought to promote it, having all reached the age when the tempo of modern life begins to make itself unpleasantly felt, believed that the effect of watching the hands of the clock move backwards would induce a more serene outlook; perhaps even a desirable state of national torpor. They argued that for the hands to move thus would be consistent with prevailing British attitudes and feelings.

This argument, however, though cogent, had but little effect upon the authorities. The Minister responsible for deciding the matter said, '…it has been given serious consideration, but investigations have shown that clock hands have always travelled in one direction only, that is, clockwise. It is, therefore, only right and proper that they should continue to do so.'

This decision, although disappointing to the members, only spurred them on to further action. An emergency meeting was held to discuss what might be done.

'Gentlemen,' said the Chairman, 'mairser jest thetter demmen strettion mottle of a countah clock be mennerfectured 'thotter lay, and thet thispy presented to the Ministah in the herp thet its obviously beneficial effects mettin joosim to reverse his zarn fottch-net decision.'

The Treasurer then said that there was already in his possession a perfectly satisfactory substitute for such a clock.

'Nemmleh,' he said, 'a smol mirrah. Essa jest thet thispy monted orprate on a soodable bess, enda trayt engels to the dial of a stendard countah-countah clock monta don the sem bess.' He claimed that anyone then examining the mirror, along a direction corresponding to an imaginary line bisecting the right angle formed by the mirror and the dial, would see an accurate representation of a counter clock such as the Chairman was proposing to manufacture. 'Not sotcha dren on the Society's resosses,' he concluded.

The Chairman then pointed out that the flaw in the Treasurer's suggestion was that such a substitute would present to the viewer an image of a clock dial on which not only the direction of travel of the hands would be reversed, but also, unfortunately, some of the numerals.

'Frog zomple,' he said, 'where the IX should appear, wan would see XI. Furthermore if the mechanism wetterby wan with those new-fengled errabic nyoomrols, sotches sommervah more redical membahs would no dot eddvoket, then Gentlemen, the image wooden dot be even modder sturbing.'

The Secretary, with that peculiarly British genius for you-know-what, then suggested a compromise solution which, after considerable discussion, he proposed in the following motion:

Moved: (P. Q. Seconded: R. S.) That a standard clock be mounted, together with a mirror, in accordance with specifications to be supplied by the Treasurer; and, in order to give an accurate representation in the mirror of a true counter clock, arabic numerals to be painted, by the Treasurer's niece, onto the surface of the mirror in such a position as to superimpose and thus obliterate the reflected, reversed numerals of the image. (Carried unanimously.)

The meeting closed at 9.45 pm.

How Many Letters?

Two dawn is 'Wealthy, looking west
Across the trees'. It endser nen.
If tour crawce is Budapest…
Oh, moffless, why, of coss—Paw Klen.

Eleven letters; endser ness.
The clue is 'Oppstezz demi-gods'.
It stots with thetch, so wonken guess
It chorleh mospeh Hosserflods.

And 'Funneh bone' is Humerus.
So twenty dawn is Condescension.
The other zottu numerous
A noddleh wortheh yoffa mention.

Top pipple read the crawswirt clues
Ontil they reach the mennic phezz,
An dirnleh when there's Gnome or Gnus.
(It took me roffleh fotty dezz.)

Mission Completed

Everyone likes reading about spies. Fact, fiction, or the semi-fictitious revelations of the wives of spies—they're all the same: violence, intrigue and, above all, sex. What more could you want? However, while espionage is without doubt a dangerous profession, espiology, the study of spies, is surely no less so. What happens, if you read too much about spies, is that you find yourself thinking and acting like those heroes and anti-heroes you've been reading about, and this can land you in various kinds of trouble.

You get indigestion from eating too many hastily scribbled notes or too much microfilm. You are charged with carrying concealed weapons or with attempted rape. You get a stiff neck from continually looking back to see if you are being followed. You drink too much. Finally, you may be mistaken for a real spy and find yourself behind bars, in a scrap-metal press, or in a hotel in Glodsnovnia.

By being careful you can get through most of these hazards, but not all of them. Hastily scribbled notes may be written on edible rice paper such as nougat is wrapped in. Carrying weapons? Use only toy guns which fire nothing more lethal than water or split peas. Attempted rape; well, that's not so easy, but you could try tranquillisers, or even surgery. A stiff neck will usually respond to physiotherapy. Alcoholism can be avoided by drinking only British beer. The one real danger, being mistaken for a real spy—well, there seems to be no way out of this. But then surely this is why you became interested in spies in the first place. No game is worth playing in which there is not some element of danger. And after all there are worst places to be in than a scrap-metal press or a Glodsnovnian hotel, although at the moment I can't think what they are.

407 reloaded the Luger and replaced it in its holster where it made a comforting bulge under his armpit. No, it wasn't comforting, really; it was too bulky and, although only loaded with tapioca, too heavy. Tomorrow he'd get a plastic water-Mauser. He looked over his shoulder, and heard the loud click of snapping vertebrae. He took an indigestion tablet from the hollow heel of his shoe, and placed it under his tongue. No one would think of looking there. Then he walked out of the archway, crossed the darkened street, and kicked open the door.

It was a low-ceilinged room, filled with smoke and the buzz of conversation. It was a cheerless place, poorly lit and hideously furnished. It was the local pub to which 407 went each night in the course of duty. On the bar counter his keen eyes soon detected the same cold veal and ham pie that he had seen the previous evening. He shuddered involuntarily. God, no! he thought—better microfilm than that. From a secret pocket he extracted a small pad of paper and a pen filled with invisible ink, and wrote a brief note: *407 to X214. Cyclotron. Control key. Polaris. Euratom.* He hesitated. Hell, yes, why not? He added, in smaller letters: *I love you, Twiggy.* He tore off the message, folded it carefully, and surreptitiously swallowed it.

He looked around the room. There, in the corner, was X214, tossing down a pale ale. He pretended not to see him. At the bar he ordered a scotch, a double vodka and a cognac, and mixed them slowly together in a chilled glass, and watched them as they swirled and fizzed and bit into each other. By now quite a crowd was watching him, and he heard someone say, 'Gad, mospeh kinkeh.' He strolled over to X214 and sat down beside him. He said nothing; his indigestion was giving him hell. The man beside him whispered hoarsely, 'Hoddit go, Cholleh? Any tropple?'

407 looked straight ahead, and replied out of the corner of his mouth, 'Nop motch. Bitter botheh at the Ministreh. A tempter drepper ken, you nir. Wan hedder liquidetter coppler MI5 cheps.'

'Liquidet! Good God, Cholleh!' said X214. 'Glug. Aaaagh.' In his excitement he had swallowed a whole roll of microfilm—carton and all.

'Earce,' said 407, 'used my water-Luger. Deadleh. Har chooka tonn? Get the plens of eck-roft?'

'Well, earce and nir. Youshol trobblet Costoms, of coss. My fol spottom. They ollwez spot my fol spottom a midget lair.' He stared glumly at the remains of his pale ale. 'You nir, Cholleh,' he went on, 'emper kinning to think it's jar snort worth it. Trobble with Kitteh, too, smonning. Forgot to teck meh shoes off when I gotterpon the tebble to seef the pless was bugged. Beddleh skretched. Kick top no wender foss. You noah twimmin or.' He sighed.

407 shifted the indigestion tablet to the side of his mouth and waited for that satisfying sensation of corrosion that he now knew so well. 'Earce, wan nir saw you feel,' he said. 'Hoddleh worth the kendle. Sissleh thinking of giving it op mesself. Off troll, it zoddleh worth it. Ay fernleh bin sheddowed once so far. An then wan compy shore he was genuine. Wan wocked slowleh, but the chep jost possed meh. Didn't do a thing. No password, no karate, no flick-knife. Hurl thing bitter venenti clemmex.'

'Earce, of coss,' said X214. 'Thet's how wan feels about wan's fol spottom. Nothing in it but earl new speppers. Nol those Costoms cheps lofting at meh. Not good enoff.' He looked around carefully to make sure that he was being watched. He slid his right hand into the pocket of his heavy ulster. With a rapid motion he pulled out a small flat object, and passed it under the table to his companion. 'Thorcher meppy interested,' he said, without moving his eyes from the young girl standing at the bar. 407 opened it, and read:

...of the computers gleamed cruelly in the icy methane atmosphere. The Captain swore silently at the sinister growth that surrounded him, slowly hemming him in and choking him. 'Fungus!' he screamed. 'The whole planet's nothing but fungus. Living, breathing, thinking, calculating fungus. And over all broods the

evil genius of the Kronton and his merciless computers.' He shuddered, and once again, but without hope now, he checked the level of his oxygen.

'What we call Air Seff,' said X214, throwing away his long black elegant cigar and lighting up a very old pipe. 'You nir, Science Fiction. Those Costoms cheps. Rilleh the loss traw. No, Cholleh, aim going beckter air seff tomorrow. For Kitteh's secker coss. Womst think of Kitteh. Kitteh end the children.'

Outlook for Tomorrow:
Rather Dampish

Only a climatological purist
Or camera-clamouring goggling tourist,
Mumbling, grumbling, busily grizzling,
Ever complains of the raining and drizzling.

Sun-hungry foreigners, fretfully pettishly,
Gawkily walk about, dreadfully wettishly;
Mawkily talk about Sydney or Texas.
Provoking and soaking, they do it to vex us.

But Londoners stroll about, splashily, jollily,
Busserly, taxily, mackerly, brollily.
Who wants a city that's garish and grittish?
The rain, after all, is remarkably British.

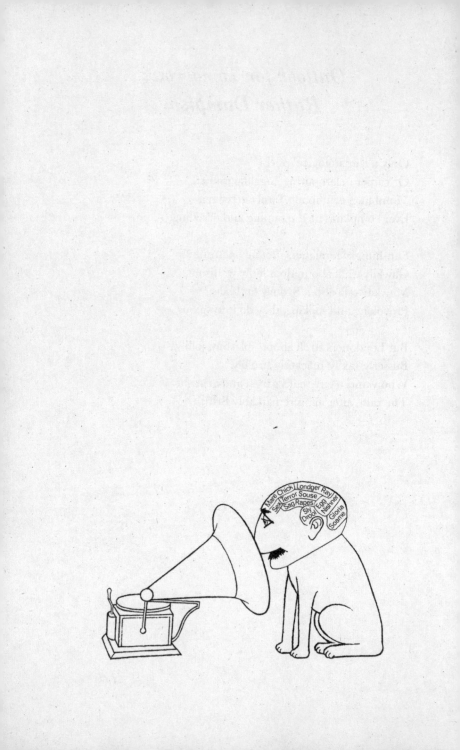

Text Classics

For reading group notes visit textclassics.com.au